Background to business

2nd Edition

15

Longman Secretarial Studies Series

Series Editor
A. R. Leal
Head of Business Studies Department
Plymouth College

A. R. Leal
MA (Cantab) LLB Grad Cert Ed AMBIM
Chief Examiner for Background to Business in the
Secretarial Studies Certificate of the London
Chamber of Commerce
Head of Business Studies Department
Plymouth College of Further Education

Background to business

2nd Edition

Longman   London and New York

Longman Group Limited,
Longman House, Burnt Mill, Harlow,
Essex CM20 2JE, England
Associated companies throughout the world

Published in the United States of America
by Longman Inc., New York

© Longman Group Limited 1979, 1984

First published 1979
Second edition 1984
Second impression 1985

British Library Cataloguing in Publication Data

Leal, A. R.
  Background to business. — 2nd ed.
  1. Commerce
  I. Title   II. Owen, W. Background to business
  380.1   HF1007
ISBN 0-582-41345-1

Printed in Great Britain at The Pitman Press, Bath

Contents

 **Series Foreword**

I am more than pleased to note that the increasing popularity of the secretarial examinations of the London Chamber of Commerce and Industry, Commercial Education Scheme, has led to a publisher feeling justified in launching a series of books specifically designed to meet our syllabus requirements.

In 1956 the Commercial Education Scheme introduced a comprehensive and progressive scheme of secretarial qualifications which now range from the Secretarial Studies Certificates, through the Private Secretary's Certificate, to the high levels of the Private Secretary's Diploma. The standards were set high, but were a realistic interpretation of the demands by employers of their employees at different points in their careers. The success of this policy is seen in the increasing numbers of candidates from centres in the UK and overseas and with the very considerable public recognition by press, radio and television when the Secretary of the Year Award is announced on the basis of the candidate achieving the best all-round success in the Private Secretary's Diploma.

May I wish all potential students every success, and hope that they and their teachers will find considerable help in this book.

R. W. Cattell, MA, FESB, MBIM

Director of the Commercial Education Scheme
London Chamber of Commerce and Industry

Preface

The completely rewritten second edition incorporates the changes in the syllabus introduced in 1983 and contains several new features.

1. Press cuttings appear throughout the main text to create more realism.

2. 'Case Study' chapters in section B which draw together material already contained in section A.

3. A brief section on model answers.

4. A sample of projects. These have always been a feature of this syllabus and the LCC is frequently consulted on their assessment. It has kindly agreed to allow two real projects to be incorporated into the book to provide guidance to students and lecturers.

5. Press cuttings at the end of the book to reinforce earlier material and assist students to keep abreast of current affairs.

Past questions appear at the end of each chapter and the text has been considerably expanded so that students can use the book with minimal guidance from the lecturer.
It is hoped these changes will make the book more readable.
The author would like to thank his wife for typing the manuscript in difficult circumstances.

Acknowledgement

We are indebted to the following for permission to reproduce copyright material:

Commercial Union Assurance for our Figs. 10.1, 10.2 and 10.3; Halifax Building Society for our Fig. 5.4; Lloyds Bank for our Figs. 5.1 and 5.2; and the London Chamber of Commerce for permission to quote questions from past examination papers and to incorporate past projects in the text.

There is a sixty-minute cassette tape, written by the Chief Examiner, accompanying this book. It expands on material in the main text and provides advice on examination techniques. The cassette, price £3.25, can be obtained by sending this form to

Barl Enterprises
Lake House
78 Radford Park Road
Plymstock
Plymouth
Devon
PL9 9DX

Please send . . . . copy/copies of the Background to Business cassette to

NAME   ....

ADDRESS   ....

   ....

I enclose a cheque for £ ....

Section A

Trade unions
Chapter 1

Types of union

In the UK there are four distinct categories of union.

Craft unions

These are open to all the skilled craftsmen in an industry irrespective of the firms they work for. They are the oldest type of union but have become less important in recent years; changes in the nature of employment have resulted in falling membership and many craft unions now allow semi-skilled or even unskilled workers to join. The craft unions are, however, still very important within the printing industry.

General unions

Membership of these is open to all regardless of their skill or the industry in which they work. Two of the largest unions in this category are the Transport and General Workers' Union and the General and Municipal Workers' Union.

Industrial unions

As the name suggests this type of union is open to all the employees within one particular industry regardless of their skill or grade. They are typical in the USA and Germany but no true industrial unions exist in the UK. The nearest are the National Union of Mineworkers and the National Union of Railwaymen. Even they do not represent all their industries' employees; the NUR for example coexists with a craft union (Associated Society of Locomotive Engineers and Firemen) and a white-collar union (Transport Salaried Staff Association).

White-collar unions

This is the fastest growing part of the trade-union movement for three reasons.

1. The loss of job security
Clerical occupations were, at one time, very secure and redundancy was unknown. Today the growth of modern technology has resulted in severe reductions in clerical areas.

Bank jobs at risk

A report on the impact of new technology in banking suggests that up to 10 per cent of existing jobs could be lost by 1990. This means that 250,000 jobs are at risk around Europe. . . .

Barclays Bank is to close 150 banking offices, including 63 full branches as part of an ambitious reshaping of its network. This makes it the first of the big four banks to announce a streamlining of its branch system, at a time when rising costs and new electronic systems have raised big question marks over the future of the huge high-street networks.

The closures will be over two years and the downgrading of the 700 branches over five to seven years. There is no redundancy programme but 350 branch managers will be offered voluntary early retirement over the five- to seven-year period "to combat any adverse impact upon promotion prospects", the bank said.

Bank unions, which were told on Friday, expressed serious concern about the career prospects for members. A spokesman for the Banking Insurance and Finance Union said it was concerned about the jobs of managers being put at risk and promotion routes being blocked. Up to a third of managers in some grades were to go.

GA jobs to dry up

General Accident, the country's largest motor insurer, is today negotiating redundancies with the unions ASTMS and Apex. There is no indication of the number of job losses and General Accident hopes that most of the jobs will go by natural wastage and early redundancies.

The need to improve efficiency has also put pressure on clerical posts.

Shell HQ jobs go

Hundreds of jobs are to be lost among the 850 employees of Shell UK Oil who work in the Shell-Mex building in the Strand, in London.

Mr. Japp Klootwijk, the managing director of Shell's marketing and refining wing in Britain, has sent a letter to staff warning that "substantial and sustainable reductions in costs" must be achieved during 1984. He has ordered all managers in the building to find ways of cutting overheads in their departments by 40 per cent.

Employees, who mostly carry out administrative functions, fear that job cuts of around 30 per cent will be ordered. "A really large change in head-office costs can only be achieved by eliminating tasks, although well-performed and desirable, but which must be seen as not absolutely essential", Mr. Klootwijk said in his circular.

2. The growth of the 'office-factory'
Many clerical staff now work with machines (albeit sophisticated electronic ones) and this has caused a change in atmosphere which has been conducive to union recruitment.

3. The loss of 'status' of white-collar workers
During the 1950s and 1960s the industrial unions achieved large pay increases for their members, longer holidays and improved working conditions. The non-union office worker failed to achieve the same improvements. Many have joined unions as a result.

Membership of a white-collar union is open to staff in non-manual occupations such as teachers, computer programmers, civil servants, supervisors and clerical staff. The union may be organised around one occupation (teachers or banks) or cover a variety of occupations.

Once you start work you would be entitled to join a white-collar union. It therefore seems appropriate to examine the organisation structure of one such union (APEX – Association of Professional, Executive Clerical and Computer Staff).

Organisation of APEX

This is a medium-sized union with approximately 150,000 members and is organised along traditional union lines. Thus the body responsible for administering the union is the **Executive Council.** This consists of:

- Representatives elected by the membership. Two representatives are elected by national ballot of all the membership while each region (of which there are nine) can nominate one representative.

- Alongside the eleven lay representatives (i.e. members who have full-time jobs) there are the full-time union officials, the most important of whom is the general secretary. He is the union's chief spokesman and the secretaries of the main unions are national figures (e.g. Arthur Scargill of the NUM).

The executive council of APEX normally meets once a month in London and its function is to implement union policy. This is laid down at the unions's **Annual Conference** by delegates from the branches of the union, each branch being entitled to send to it one delegate for each 50 of its members. Because branches have stronger representation at their conferences white-collar unions are considered more democratic than general unions.

Prior to the conference proposals for consideration at it are submitted by branches to the executive council; such branch proposals are circulated to all branches to give them an opportunity to discuss them and to make recommendations on voting to their appointed delegates.

At conference the delegate's role is to discuss and debate the proposals on the agenda, bearing in mind the recommendations of their branch but often relying heavily upon the advice of the executive council and of full-time officials. Votes are taken and these are binding on the executive council.

Below the executive council are the geographical regions. One of these covers the West of England and it is administered by a lay regional council. Its role is mainly administrative, the effective power being wielded by the full-time paid official (the area secretary) who has his own full-time officers. His function is to serve the membership within his region and he is responsible to the general secretary of the union.

Role of the full-time local union officer

The full-time officers responsible to the area secretary would spend most of their time in the 'branches'. When visiting them the officer may:
1. Negotiate with management in instances where local representatives have been unsuccessful in resolving a specific grievance involving a union member. When this happens a 'failure to agree' is registered and the full-time official is called in to deal with the problem.
2. Negotiate with management over pay settlements. In some companies the **staff representative (shop steward)** negotiates on behalf of the members but frequently the negotiations are left to the full-time official.
3. Discuss union policy with members.
4. Attend meetings of staff representatives to talk about union objectives and the tactics they should use in pursuing these.
5. Recruit members.

The branch and unpaid officers

We have already mentioned the **Branch** in connection with the annual conference. Every union member belongs to a branch which is based either on one company or on companies in a small geographical area. The branch holds regular meetings (although attendance at such meetings is usually low) and elects a committee. Most branch committees are comprised of staff representatives (in some unions called 'shop stewards') who are appointed representatives of members working in local companies.

The staff representative is unpaid (although the firm may give time off to perform trade union functions) and is expected to deal with local union matters. Thus the official may:

- act as a negotiator with management;
- seek to increase union membership;
- act as a communications link between the members and the full-time officials;
- represent the union on committees;
- monitor health and safety standards (in many white-collar unions the function of staff representative and health and safety representative are separated);
- collect union dues.

Aims and objectives of a union

A union exists to represent its members and therefore its aims are those of its members. As the immediate priorities of members change so the short-term objectives of the union must change. Thus in the 1970s there was considerable discussion on industrial democracy; this means giving the work-force more say in the running of the company by perhaps having representatives on the board of directors. In the 1980s much less is heard about this as most unions seem preoccupied with pay and unemployment (which with unemployment figures in excess of 3,000,000 in 1985 is hardly surprising) as the following articles show.

In a switch of policy the General Municipal and Boilermakers' Union[1] conference next weekend will be asked to support the idea of a statutory minimum wage to underpin union attempts to eradicate low pay.

It stresses that sympathetic government action must be paralleled by a concerted commitment by unions to give low pay priority in their bargaining and organisational activities.

Note

1. **This is a general union.**

The executive of the Transport & General Workers' Union[1] voted yesterday to ban from March 1983 the importation of the Vauxhall "S" car, the new General Motors small model already being marketed on the Continent as the Opel Corsa.[2]

Mr. Moss Evans, the union's general secretary, said that it was taking a stand against imports which now accounted for 55 per cent of car sales in Britain.[3]

"No country can afford to import cars at the rate of 50 to 55 per cent", said Mr. Evans, "If the Government is not prepared to deal with a serious situation where the fabric of the motor vehicle industry is being destroyed, then we have got to do something. . . . "We cannot afford to allow our members to be put on the dole. We have warned Vauxhall repeatedly but they have just ignored us".

Notes

1. The TGWU is a general union.
2. A ban on imports is a form of industrial action.
3. Imports now account for 55 per cent of car sales (refer to Ch. 6).

The changing priorities of union members can be explained by the work of Maslow who was an industrial psychologist.* He analysed individual needs and classified them into five groups as illustrated in Fig. 1.1.

Fig. 1.1

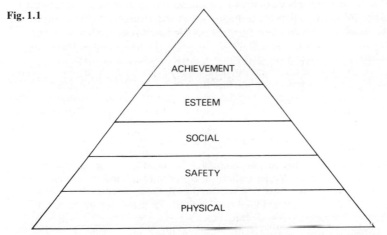

* The work of other industrial psychologists is discussed in the tape accompanying this book.

According to Maslow an individual starts at the bottom of the triangle and seeks to satisfy physical needs. *Only* when these have been satisfied can there be a move up the triangle to 'safety'. Thus once a need is satisfied you move up to the next one. To put it simply, if you are starving you are solely preoccupied with finding food (physical) and don't care what your neighbours think of you (esteem).

Physical needs are self-explanatory; they include food and shelter. *Safety* needs could be described as security; office workers want to feel secure in their employment (no fear of redundancy, etc.). In the 1970s there was job security, wages were rising and promotion prospects were healthy. The bottom two needs in the triangle were satisfied and so individuals started to look at levels three, four and five. These are more difficult to explain but involve the employee feeling 'part of the organisation' with the capacity to 'achieve' something (to obtain job satisfaction). By the 1980s the fear of redundancy had increased to such an extent that employees' safety needs were unmet. The satisfaction of these then became paramount and the work-force soon lost interest in the higher needs.

It follows therefore that the aims a union may pursue at a moment in time will vary. In the long term, however, it is possible to classify the main aims of unions. Before this is done let us eavesdrop on a meeting at which the local union official is trying to persuade clerical and secretarial staff to join APEX.

Official
'I accept that most people don't join unions simply because they think it's a good thing. They usually join because we can help with a particular problem. Perhaps they are unhappy with their level of pay (most people still assume this is our main function) or their working conditions. Office workers have complained to me about draughts, lack of carpeting, lack of heating and even canteen facilities. You'd be surprised at their problems. People may join, not because they have specific problems, but because they have a feeling that their point of view is not being considered by management and there is a general lack of consultation. They want somebody who can make their voice heard and inform them as to what is going on.

'Once we are recognised by the firm we can solve these types of problem. You may think, "well, I'll get these benefits even if I don't join the union". That may be true but if everybody adopted that approach there'd be no union! You are also ignoring what I call the individual benefits of being a member. What are these? Well, we offer "fringe benefits" such as discount facilities with various firms, cheap holidays, cheap car insurance, social clubs, etc., but more important we will provide you with "individual protection". Imagine you have an individual complaint or grievance. You may be afraid to mention it to your employer or lack the expertise to pursue it (especially if it involves the complex employment legislation). The union official has the expertise and also the access to senior management. You may have, even in the office, a problem with health and safety ranging from eye strain with visual display units to (surprisingly) potential risks with the use of certain chemicals. The union has extensive research facilities on office-related health and safety issues and is therefore in a position to give sound advice. Another individual benefit arises if you "get into trouble" and you are subject to disciplinary hearings. The union will represent you and while it might agree to your dismissal it will insist the appropriate procedures are followed.

'Being in a union is almost like taking out insurance in case a problem occurs. The union will even provide you with legal aid and advice; this is particularly important as regards accidents at work. If the management contest the case you will not be able to afford to take it to court. The union will, however, pay legal costs in approved cases.'

The above enables us to summarise the main aims of a union thus:
1. To improve conditions at work.
2. To improve job security.
3. To improve the working environment.

To achieve these aims unions negotiate with employers; they indulge in collective bargaining. Each seeks to obtain the best deal although both parties must of course work within the legal framework. Thus in some trades the employers cannot negotiate a lower wage than the statutory minimum (i.e. laid down in law) and all contracts must conform to Acts of Parliament such as the Contracts of Employment Act.

The white-collar unions generally are less militant than their industrial colleagues (white-collar unions do not use the term 'brother'!) arguing that they achieve success through logical argument rather than by industrial muscle. Occasionally, however they do get involved in strikes.

Ford managers are to meet leaders of the white-collar union ASTMS in London today to try to resolve the strike by 550 foremen and supervisors which has prevented car production since Monday at the Halewood plant in Liverpool.	The dispute hinges on responsibility for training workers on the production line.[1] Ford says that the foreman's responsibilities include job instruction, with physical demonstration when required.

Note

1. This provides an illustration of on-the-job training (see Ch. 3)

The manual unions are more likely to be involved in industrial action (although this is not as common as would appear from media presentation). While the more common forms of industrial action can include strikes, sit-ins, and working-to-rule, other forms of industrial action can also be used.

Strikes

British Leyland's first crisis since the departure of Sir Michael Edwardes deepened yesterday when 1,700 men had to be sent home as a direct result of a strike by 5,000 workers at Cowley over the withdrawal of so-called "washing up time".

The dispute has come at an embarrassing time for BL, less than a month after the launch of the Maestro. This is a success in the showrooms, and some 6,200 Maestros have been sold in the last four weeks. However, 20,000 vehicles have been produced, so stockpiles are high. . . .

The strike, costing the company 800 vehicles a day in lost production, left management and unions with little common ground last night, and all the signs are that it will continue over the holiday period. . . .

The shop stewards continued to claim yesterday that the overwhelming votes in favour of a strike reflected not only dissatisfaction over the company's latest move but also anger over the way manning levels and work practices have been altered in the past year or so.

Sit-ins

Britain's world lead in flat TV screen technology is being jeopardised by the sit-in at the Timex Dundee plant. Clive Sinclair, the inventor of the best-selling personal computer, is close to cancelling the project if the dispute is not settled quickly.

Crisis talks take place in Glasgow today between Scottish industry minister Alex Fletcher and union leaders. Last night Fletcher, alarmed at the damage to Scotland's reputation as a high technology investment location, said: "The whole future of the Timex plant is under threat. Time is running out."

Fletcher called the union meeting after Sinclair – whose computer is made at the Timex factory

– travelled to London last week to deliver what amounted to an ultimatum. The five-week-old sit-in, in protest over planned job losses by Timex management, is costing Sinclair £1m a week. Despite desperate efforts by Sinclair managers, the Timex workers are refusing to allow work on the vital cathode ray tube for Sinclair's £50 mini-TV, due to be launched this summer. . . .

With the Japanese about to launch their own mini-TV, Sinclair believes that his lead is fast being eroded. "We can't afford to delay", said a spokesman for Sinclair last night. "We may have to drop the project altogether if we don't hit the market at the right time."

Work-to-rule

Warders' strike sparks 4-hour noise protest at Dartmoor

More than 500 prisoners in Dartmoor gaol staged a four-hour protest of banging tin mugs, whistling, singing, and shouting yesterday because of conditions caused by a prison officers' work-to-rule. . . .

Prisoners have had no exercise periods outdoors for nearly three weeks and no association with others. . . .

The amount of time spent in their cells, each of which is occupied by only one man, has also been substantially increased as a result of the "controlled unlocking" – any one prison officer will only unlock three prisoners at a time, when previously about 30 would have been unlocked. . . .

Visits from outside are also believed to have been suspended almost completely, and all chapel visits cancelled. Workshop hours and visits to the canteen have been severely curtailed.

Mr. David Evans, general secretary of the Prison Officers Association, said that everything in the prison was taking several times as long, and prisoners were having to spend about 10 times as long in their cells each day. . . .

Prison officers were working according to regulations in protest at recent cuts in manning levels imposed by the Home Office.

Of course there are numerous other ways to disrupt a company.

Vauxhall men at Luton lift ban on Spanish car

Vauxhall's 7,500 workers at Luton voted yesterday to call off their ban on imports of the Spanish Nova in return for a resumption of night-shift production.

Yesterday's vote follows talks between national union officials and Vauxhall directors last week. The company has agreed to increase line production rates, leading to a return to double shifts at Luton in August. . . .

The package also includes agreements on early retirement and voluntary severance. The

unions are hoping that enough of the older staff will volunteer for early retirement to guarantee jobs for apprentices at the end of their training.

"The unions' requirements for allowing the Spanish car in were a return to double shifting, which the company has conceded", said a spokesman for the Amalgamated Union of Engineering Workers. "Our recommendation was to accept the outcome of the talks between our national officials and the company directors."

Industrial action should be the last resort and where the employers and unions cannot agree they may request the assistance of a third party to help solve the dispute.

Ford yesterday accepted an independent inquiry finding that Mr. Paul Kelly, an assembly worker at the Halewood, Liverpool, plant should not have been dismissed for allegedly deliberately damaging a bracket. He should instead have been suspended for 10 days without pay, given written warning, and transferred to another section.

The dismissal in March led to a strike by 5,000 Halewood workers. Mr. Kelly, who has been suspended on basic pay, will now be offered a new job. . . .

The inquiry, which was headed by Mr. John Wood, chairman of the Central Arbitration Committee clearly felt the bending of a bracket should become a sackable offence only after a written warning.

The value of having assistance from an independent third party was recognised by the creation in 1974 of the Advisory, Conciliation and Abitration Service (ACAS).

ACAS

As its name suggests it has three main functions. It advises employers and unions on any matters concerned with industrial relations; this service is free. The conciliation service involves persuading the parties to a dispute to talk to each other; it has been defined as 'the act of promoting goodwill between people'. It is hoped that by persuading the parties to discuss their problem in a friendly atmosphere a solution is more likely. Arbitration usually occurs when both sides disagree and cannot see any possibility of a solution. It arises when they ask a third party (ACAS) to make a decision which both sides will accept. (ACAS does not itself arbitrate but nominates a third party.)

ACAS to mediate in vandal strike

The three-week-old strike at Ford's Halewood plant over allegations of vandalism by an assembly worker is to go to ACAS for arbitration, the company and unions agreed yesterday.

The above article refers to the dispute outlined earlier where the arbitrator was chairman of the Central Arbitration Committee.

If the parties are not prepared to accept binding arbitration ACAS can arrange mediation. This involves getting the two parties together with a third party who puts forward proposals for discussion or acceptance. The parties are, however free to ignore any recommendations he makes, unlike arbitration.

Trades Union Congress

Almost every union belongs to the TUC. Just as employees benefit by joining together so the unions benefit by having one body representing all the unions in negotiations with employers and the government. The head of the TUC is the general secretary but, although he exercises considerable influence, he is bound by the policy laid down by the Annual Congress. Delegates to this represent all the affiliated unions and apart from determining policy elect the General Council who are responsible for implementing policy. It works through committees (supported by full-time staff) on which members of the council sit; details of the main committees and membership (1983) are found in the following article.

The centre-right majority on the enlarged TUC General Council is to be mirrored in all its major committees under a distribution of seats agreed yesterday by senior members.

The new members of the *finance and general purposes committee* are Mr. Rodney Bickerstaff, of Nupe; Mr. Tony Christopher of the Inland Revenue Staff Federation; Mr. Jack Eccles (General Municipal and Boilermakers); Mr. Ken Gill, of the white-collar engineers Tass; Mr. Bill Sirs (iron and steel workers); Mr. Bill Whatley (shop-workers); and Mr. Les Wood (building workers).

Mr. Bickerstaffe will also serve on the *economic committee* with Mr. Ray Buckton, of Aslef, Mr. John Daly, general secretary-elect of Nalgo, Mr. Alastair Graham, of the Civil and Public Services Association, Mr. Alex Smith (tailors and garment workers), Mr. Alan Tuffin (communication workers), and Ms Muriel Turner, of the Association of Scientific, Technical, and Managerial Staffs.

New members of the *employment committee,* which meets Mr. Norman Tebbit on Thursday over his trade union democracy proposals, are Mr. Roy Grantham, of the clerical union Apex: Mr. Eric Hammond, general secretary-elect of the electricians; Mr. Bryan Stanley (post office engineers); Mrs Lil Stevens (Nupe); and Mr. Joe Wade, of the print union NGA.

Mr. Graham, Mr. Gill, Mr. Tuffin, and Mr. Whatley go on the *international committee* with Miss Ada Maddocks, of Nalgo, Mr. John Morton, of the Musicians' Union, Mr. Gerry Russell, of the AUEW, and Mr. David Williams, of the health union Cohse.

The committees are responsible for the day-to-day work and report on their progress to the regular council meetings.

The TUC can intervene in industrial disputes involving member unions; these are not always union v. employer as is shown in the following article.

> The TUC has been asked to intervene in a bitter inter-union conflict over who should represent more than 5,000 managers in ICI and other top chemical firms. One of the most savage white-collar recruitment wars of recent years has come to a head with a complaint by Frank Chapple's electricians' union against ASTMS.

The members of the Council sit on various bodies, such as the NEDC, as well as being involved in less formal discussions with employers and government.

Confederation of British Industry

This is the employers counterpart of the TUC and acts as industry's spokesman. You will note that in many of the press clippings the views of the CBI are mentioned.

Postscript

Female workers tend not to be unionised. Could that be the reason for the figures shown in table 1.1.?

Table 1.1 Women's pay as % of men's pay (Europe)

Country	%
Sweden	87.3
Denmark	85.5
Italy	81.5
Norway	79.8
France	75.7
Netherlands	75.0
Finland	74.3
West Germany	72.3
Belgium	71.0
Great Britain	70.0
Switzerland	66.1

Examination questions

1.

Trades Union Congress
|
Executive Committees
|
District Committees
|
Branches
|
Shop stewards
|
Members

(a) Briefly explain this simplified diagram of trade union organisation.
(b) Explain the essential differences between the following types of unions:
    (i) Craft union
    (ii) Industrial union
    (iii) White-collar unions
    (iv) General unions

(Q. 10 1977)

2. What are the main functions of shop stewards?

(Q. 3 1975)

3. A newspaper article commented that 'white-collar workers will exercise greater economic strength in the future'. Who are the white-collar workers?

(Q. 1(c) 1974)

4. Give **two** examples of issues which might be the subject of 'collective bargaining'.

(Q. 1(j) 1977)

5. What is the meaning of the terms:
    (a) conciliation
    (b) arbitration?

(Q. 1(f) 1975)

6. Describe the main objectives of a trade union and explain which you would consider most important at the present time.

(Q. g 1982)

7. Other than strikes, state two forms of disruptive action.

(Q. 1(f) 1983)

8. A large engineering concern is forced to make part of its work force redundant.
    (a) What is meant by redundancy?
    (b) Explain the ways in which a union might respond to this.
    (c) Where might the redundant staff retrain or learn new employment skills?

(Q. 8 1983)

Communications – motivation

Chapter 2

If my secretary produces a letter from the shorthand notes which I have dictated to her, this could be quoted as an example of effective communications. That is: I have communicated the content of the letter to my secretary. She has responded by producing a mailable letter. If this were all that 'communications' involved the subject would hardly merit the attention it receives on management training courses. Being an effective communicator, however, involves more than the mere ability to transmit information to another party.

In training somebody to be an efficient communicator (i.e. able to transmit information) the tutor's first task is to persuade the student to answer the question, 'what does the other party (e.g. staff) need to know?' This will enable her to determine the content of the communication. The first essential in communicating is therefore to decide on the information you need to give the other party.

- If you are seeking a quotation for the installation of computers in your office then you must tell the supplier the number of terminals you require, the memory capability, the job they must perform, etc. A letter simply asking for a quote for a computer system would be meaningless.

- If I want my secretary to type a letter with two copies, then I must tell her.

- If I want a report typed in double spacing so as to allow correction, then I must inform the typist, otherwise it will be typed with normal spacing.

- If I give the operator a document for the word processor, she will need to be told about the number of copies I want and whether I require the document to be stored on a 'floppy disk'.

- If a new piece of equipment arrives, then before I ask staff to use it, they must receive clear instructions on how to operate it.

A lecturer must decide what information she is going to give the students during the lesson. She has to answer the question, 'What do the students need to know to pass their examinations?' At some time during your schooling you will probably have left a class having failed to understand the lesson. There has been a failure in communication. It may have occurred because your teacher tried to tell you too much. In business it is equally important not to 'overload' the staff with information, as the sheer volume of it may only serve to confuse them. The more you tell someone the more they are likely to forget something. For this reason when communicating try to be precise and to the point (without being so brief you don't make sense). You must therefore be careful not to give information which is irrelevant. If a new computer arrives in the office, then a brief description of its functions will probably suffice. No purpose is served in explaining how the computer operates with detailed descriptions of its circuitry.

Having given the information you must check that the recipient has understood it. The college lecturer will check that her students have understood the lesson by asking them questions or perhaps getting them to write an essay. In business you cannot ask the staff to write an essay but you can ask them to repeat the instructions or, if you have instructed them how to operate a new piece of equipment, you can watch them use it the first time.

The above deals with the 'mechanical' side of communications but an effective communicator can use her skills to **'motivate'** the staff. The communications process can be used to make staff feel part of the organisation; they will respond by working harder. What is communicated and **how** it is communicated can be important in motivating staff. My secretary will type a letter whether I say 'type that letter' or 'please type that letter'. The choice of instruction will, however, affect her attitude and her commitment to the business.

The key to motivating staff is to remember that they are human. They have feelings and provided you respect these you will gain the respect of the staff. Therefore:

1. Explain to your staff why
It is part of human nature to want to know why things happen or why an instruction has been given. Suppose the letter dictated, which was mentioned in the earlier example, said:

Dear Mr Johnson,
Thank you for your application for the recently advertised post. I regret to inform you that on this occasion you have not been successful.
Yours faithfully

Successfully dictating the letter means successful communication, but it is hardly going to motivate the secretary. A good employer may therefore discuss the reason for the decision with his secretary after dictating the letter. He may explain that the person was too old or perhaps insufficiently qualified. The secretary now knows the reason for the decision and this will help broaden her experience.

I may want the caretaker to move two additional typing desks into a classroom. If, after the request, I say **'because** our classes are 22 instead of the 20 we planned', he knows the reason for the request. If when you give an order (or preferably make a request – 'please would you . . .') you always say **because** you will satisfy the other person's desire to know why.

2. When communicating use the most appropriate method or medium.
When the communicator concerned with motivation decides on the method of communicating she must appreciate:
(a) *The difference between one-way and two-way communications.*
The latter allows a response from the employee whereas the former does not. **One-way** communication such as a notice board or a firm's weekly bulletin is therefore useful for giving out information such as the time of a meeting, a staff dance, winner of a competition or the basic facts on a new product. Where, however, the staff are likely to want to ask questions, it is better to use **two-way** communications such as an interview or a meeting. If an employer wants to ask his office staff to work late for a week to produce his accounts, then the request is much better done at a meeting where the staff can ask questions. If the request is simply put on a notice board then such questions cannot be answered and this leads to speculation and the development of a 'grapevine'.
(b) *The formal channels of communication.* Most organisations possess a formal channel of communications. Thus if I want a junior member of my office staff to perform a task I would be expected to go through the office manager and not go directly to the person concerned. People tend to get upset if they are by-passed; it can suggest a lack of confidence in them, and this affects their morale.

In many organisations the formal channels of communication can be found by examining the **organisation chart**. Communication within a typical College of Further Education could be along the lines shown in Fig. 2.1.

Fig. 2.1

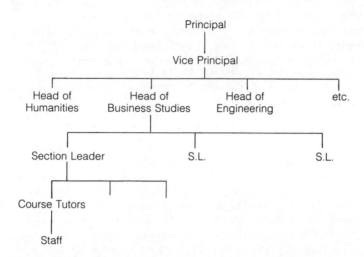

The figure shows that it is the Head of Department who is responsible for passing information from the Principal to the staff. He would, however, be expected in most cases to do this via his Section Leaders. It is they who are the link between the Head and his staff. In theory a link therefore exists between the Principal and his staff.

If a Section Leader in Humanities wanted to discuss a problem with her counterpart in Business Studies (perhaps over the teaching of communications), then if she used the channels in the chart, she would mention it to her Head who would talk to the Head of Business Studies. This process would be cumbersome. In the organisation there will therefore be a formal system of **lateral (sideways)** communication so that Section Leaders can communicate directly with each other.

We have seen that a one-way communication, such as a noticeboard, will be inappropriate when the staff may have questions. In deciding the method of communication we were considering the **'needs'** of the staff. The **'feelings'** of a member of staff may also be relevant in determining the way we communicate.

Some information of a private or confidential nature is best dealt with on a one-to-one basis.

> My Secretary might arrive ten minutes late for work on several occasions. I may feel the need to talk to her. Our interview is best conducted in private. An interview will be chosen because she may wish to say something and it will be held in private because criticism in front of her colleagues is likely to lead to resentment on her part and a lowering of morale. This could ultimately lead to a less effective secretary.

3. Think how your staff will react. Important letters should not be dictated immediately after the Christmas office party! Your secretary's shorthand may be rather shaky. Seriously, the timing is important because it can affect the staff response. Returning to an earlier example, I want my office staff to put in some overtime. I decide quite correctly that the request should be made at a meeting and choose Friday at 4.15 p.m., fifteen minutes before they go home. The previous week has been difficult, because of pressure of work, and by 4.15 p.m. on Friday staff are anxious to go home. It would therefore not be surprising if my request for overtime received an unfavourable reply.

My secretary may have improved considerably since the interview we had regarding her poor time-keeping, and being a good employer I may wish to congratulate her. I inform her on Friday at 4.30 p.m. just as she is about to leave that I wish to see her in my office on Monday at 9.00 a.m. What is the effect of this piece of information? My secretary is likely to spend the weekend worrying about why I want to see her. She may feel that there is going to be another critical interview. By choosing an inappropriate time to notify her of the interview, I have created tension for her over the weekend and illustrated a lack of awareness of staff feelings. If you wish to see a member of staff, it is much better to make an appointment for the same day.

It was mentioned earlier that you must check that your communication has been understood, perhaps by asking questions. This involves you **listening** to the reply. The ability to listen is also vital in motivating staff. If staff come to you with their problems they want to feel you are listening to them. The manager who is too busy or appears to be thinking of other more important matters while staff are talking is likely to give them the impression that they are unimportant. This will hardly improve their performance in the office. What this means is that if you are genuinely interested in your staff they are more likely to respond by working harder. If your secretary asks for time off to take her daughter to the dentist an enquiry the next day as to how the visit went may result in a better relationship with your secretary.

You should also be prepared to listen when staff have ideas about improving the business. If you apparently ignore them they will feel you consider their views unimportant.

As a good communicator you will realise how important your staff are and go out of your way to reassure them of their importance. You will say 'thank you' when they do something well and be lavish in your praise. Individuals love to be praised and it generally produces a good reaction from them. You should be slow to criticise but quick to praise, and if possible call them by their name. (If you have any doubts on the wisdom of this just think how you feel when your lecturer praises you!)

The above may seem simple but in reality poor communications

exists throughout large parts of British Industry. Just read the
following article.

British Leyland Cars last night claimed that 3,000 men who voted for a strike which stopped all production, including the Maestro, at Cowley had been misled by union officials.

The men walked out after being told at a mass meeting that management was adamant that "washing up periods" had to be swallowed by the working day to allow production lines to be kept running to the end of each shift. This would add another 66 minutes or 100 cars to the working week.

BL claimed that the men had been misled because the three minutes, twice a day in the morning and the evening, and a total of nine minutes a day on the night shift, customarily taken off so that workers could wash themselves, had no official basis.

The workers see the move as another change in working practices, of which they claim they have had to endure many during the past two years. Mr. Bobby Fryer, a senior shop steward of the Transport and General Workers'
Union said: "The decision shows just how Cowley workers are fed up with the way they have been treated."

Management said yesterday that Cowley, which produces 4,000 cars a week, including models such as the Maestro, the Acclaim and the Ambassador, was merely being brought into line with other BL car plants in the UK.

In its statement the company said: "There is no need or justification for employees of the Cowley assembly plant to be on strike. Indeed, it is very doubtful that such a decision would have been taken if they had not been advised wrongly at the mass meeting that the issue was some sort of attack on basic trade union rights. The facts are that the workers are paid to work right up to the proper finishing time. Early finishing is entirely an unofficial practice."

BL last night urged shop stewards to call another mass meeting for today saying that a proper return to work was vital to secure Cowley's future.

Two reasons why communication can be poor are given below.

1. Size of the organisation

As organisations grow in size so the number of layers of management
between the top management and the staff at the bottom grows. If a
college gets very large there may be Faculty Heads between the Vice
Principal and the Heads of Department; there may be Course Leaders.
Each layer of management means one more level through which a
communication must pass. This increases the chance of distortion and
the possibility that the communication will not get passed on. If a
student's parent telephones the Principal with a message it is most
unlikely the student will receive it, given the number of people it must
pass through! This is probably one of the reasons for the
communication problem at British Leyland. One remedy for this is to

create committees on which individuals from each of the layers of management sit. Another possibility is to divide an organisation into autonomous (separate) parts, each being of a more manageable size.

This may be preferable to the 'committee' solution because smaller units make motivation easier. In larger organisations employees can become isolated from management and this makes motivation more difficult. Communications tend to be through memos, noticeboards and magazines which, apart from being one-way communications, are impersonal. Verbal communications tend to be 'friendlier' than cold bits of paper.

2. Attitudes

To be a good motivator you must care about your staff (or persuade them that you do). Where staff have the wrong attitude the motivator's communications are more likely to create resentment than motivate. I can recall one manager who said 'Good morning' in such a way that it sounded like a question or a challenge! We have already seen how a request is far more effective than an order.

A superior who is incapable of assessing staff reaction is likely to use words his or her staff do not understand and will not appreciate how the staff will react to the message. Realising that staff prejudices and assumptions affect how they receive the message is one factor which determines how you put your message across. For instance, you might tell one manager that an order has been cancelled and his reaction will be to look for replacement orders. If the same information is given to another manager, who is less confident, he may interpret this as a hint that he is about to be made redundant.

Informal communication

Where problems exist within the formal structure because of the organisation's size or the attitude of the communicators, then there is likely to be a growth in informal channels. The most significant and perhaps the most distrusted of these is the **'grapevine'** which consists of part rumour, part gossip and occasionally part truth. Management dislike the grapevine because they cannot control it and information can become distorted. Where staff are kept fully informed there is no need for a grapevine, but where management are reluctant to tell their staff what is happening, then it is inevitable that they will speculate. If a word processor is being introduced into an office it is inevitable that staff will be concerned about possible redundancies. Managers who are aware of the problem will have a meeting with the staff to explain the impact of the word processor and reassure them. If, however, they do not bother to communicate this information with them, then the grapevine will turn the introduction of the word processor into a number of redundancies. The managers then have a problem which has arisen simply because of their failure to be aware of the importance of communication.

Examination questions

1. The larger the organisation the more difficult effective communications become. Why should this be so? What steps might be taken to minimise the risk of ineffective communications in the large organisation?

    (Q. 9   1977)

2. We often read in newspapers about 'breakdown of communications between management and workers'. What methods might be employed to improve such communications?

    (Q. 9   1976)

3. In communications what do you understand by the 'grapevine'.

    (Q. 1(f)   1983)

4. Your Personnel Department has been asked by the Board of Management to run courses for supervisors on 'effective communication'.
    (a) What might be included in the course?
    (b) Apart from training, list the other functions of a Personnel Department.

    (Q. 3   1983)

5. Give an example of one-way communication and explain when it could be used.

    (Q. 1(a)   1982)

Training

Chapter 3

Almost everyone in employment has undergone some form of training. This ranges from several years for a solicitor or accountant to a few days or even hours for Saturday staff in a large store. The amount of training you require to obtain the necessary skills, and the way in which you acquire these skills depends on the nature of your job and the type of organisation you work for.

This is illustrated if we examine the training requirements of the members of an imaginary family. Apart from the parents, Ken and Marie, there are four children, all of whom are about to leave full-time education. The eldest, Andrea, has just graduated from university with a degree in Business Studies. The other three are triplets. Derek has obtained four good 'O' levels, Evelyn passed one 'O' level and achieved two CSE grade 1's while Justine failed to pass any examinations, being more preoccupied with members of the opposite sex in her last year at school. Let us now consider each of these.

Andrea

Having obtained her degree she has decided to qualify as a Chartered Accountant. This involves further examinations (although her degree exempts her from some of the examinations). How can she obtain the tuition she needs to pass these?

Many professions (and skilled trades) insist that new entrants possess both theoretical and practical knowledge. The former can be tested through examinations but practical knowledge comes only through experience. The Chartered Accountants will therefore insist that Andrea works for a member firm (to obtain the practical knowledge) while she prepares herself for the final examinations. She will work under the close supervision of a qualified accountant who will be able to relate her theoretical knowledge to practical problems. As

she will be working full-time, tuition for a prospective Chartered
Accountant is only available in two forms:

(a) Day release
Some organisations are prepared to release their employees for one
day a week to attend a relevant course (often at a local college). This is
common with professions such as bankers. This method is expensive to
employers as they are losing their employees for one day per week
while still paying their wages.

(b) Correspondence course
This avoids the above problem as the staff do not require time off to
follow a correspondence course. Andrea can enrol with one of the
many 'correspondence colleges' who will send her books and notes
with a schedule of work. She will complete her assignments and return
them to the 'college'. Their staff will mark them and return them to
Andrea. This method is popular with employers but less popular with
employees because it involves giving up their own time in the evenings.

To 'share the burden' of tuition some employers allow staff an
afternoon off to attend college provided the staff attend on an evening
in their own time.

Derek

He has applied for, and been successful in obtaining, an 'electronics
apprenticeship' with a local firm. Like Andrea he needs to obtain both
practical and theoretical knowledge but he is fortunate in that
apprenticeships traditionally incorporate **off-the-job training,**
usually day release at the local college. When we use the term 'off-
the-job' training this indicates that training occurs away from the
normal working environment. This could be at the local college or in
the firm's own training establishment which could be just one room set
aside for training within the factory (shop or office).
   Being trained away from the work-place means he can learn in a
more relaxed environment without the noise and bustle which occurs
there. It is also easier for his tutor who is free to concentrate on
teaching; where training is given in the work-place the employee
responsible for passing on the skills has her own job to perform and
may resent the time needed to help the trainee. The employee may
also be a poor teacher, perhaps lacking the communications skills!
Lecturers are chosen for their skills and so should be more effective!
   As far as Derek is concerned he will attend a college for one day a
week to learn his theory and will spend the other four days at work
gaining practical knowledge.
   At the end of his apprenticeship he acquires 'craft' status; he is now a
tradesman (he can become a 'full' member of the appropriate craft
union).

Evelyn

She intends to become a secretary and her parents have considered both a full-time college course and a job as an office junior/receptionist.

Some skills can be taught **on-the-job;** this means an employee learns to do her job during the ordinary working day. On-the-job training would be suitable for a receptionist who was being taught to use the firm's switchboard (provided, of course, it was fairly simple and she had correct telephone techniques). Suppose you gain employment as a receptionist at your local radio station. Experience on their switchboard would be necessary. Your training on the first day would consist of three parts:

(a) You would watch the existing receptionist operate the switchboard. While using it she would explain its operation to you.
(b) You would then use the switchboard under the supervision of the receptionist.
(c) Having successfully operated the switchboard under supervision you would be left to use it on your own.

This area is suitable for on-the-job training because the new employee needs to learn on the firm's equipment and it would be costly to duplicate this facility in a training room.

Some skills cannot be learnt on the job. Consider typing. Can you imagine learning to type while watching a secretary? How could you work (i.e. type) and learn to type at the same time? If this sounds impossible imagine learning shorthand in anything other than a classroom environment. Evelyn's parents have decided that shorthand is still essential if their daughter is to obtain a worthwhile job with good promotion prospects and so they opt for a college course. This is full-time and has been designed following consultation with many of the local employers. This should ensure that students are, at the end of the course, employable. For this reason it includes both word- and information-processing. There is no cost to Evelyn's parents as education is provided by the Local Education Authority (which is primarily financed through rates paid on property and from government grants). It is unlikely that Evelyn will receive a grant to attend college (unlike Andrea who automatically received a grant at University) unless there is financial hardship within the family as might occur if her parents were unemployed, or it was a 'single-parent' family.

Evelyn could opt for a full-time course at a private college. This exists, unlike local authority colleges, to make a profit and she will therefore have to pay fees. In the UK private colleges can be found in areas other than secretarial; they exist in accountancy, data processing and teaching English to overseas students.

Justine

She has realised her mistake in choosing boys rather than books and is keen to make amends. She also applied to the local college but because of her poor school record she has been rejected. Employers have also turned down her job applications for the same reason. She is one of the unemployed.

All the political parties agree that some educational and training provision should be available to those who fail to obtain employment or a place in full-time education. In 1982 the government therefore set up a **Youth Training Scheme** (YTS). This lasts for one year and those entering it receive a training allowance; this is more than they would receive if they were on unemployment benefit but is below current wage levels. During the period of training the 'trainees' are 'employed' by a firm (the 'sponsors') and released for a period of approximately sixty-five days 'off-the-job' training. In some areas firms are using the YTS scheme to replace their first-year apprenticeship (because the government pays the cost of training and the trainees' 'wages'). At the end of the year's training the trainees may be taken on by the firm but in most cases they will leave and, unless they can find a full-time job, join the numbers of unemployed.

Justine has obtained a position with her local council. During her off-the-job training she is being taught to type, and receives a very basic grounding in computers, communications and numeracy. This is being done by the council in their own training suite although it could use the facilities provided by the local college of further education or by the private colleges in the area.

Marie

Now the children have left home their mother has decided to return to work, but having last worked 23 years ago (before she had Andrea) she requires retraining. She cannot use the local college because, being over 19, she would have to pay tuition fees and it is unlikely she would receive a grant to cover these and her living expenses.

This is a typical problem for 'mature' people wishing to retrain either because they have not worked for a long time or because they wish to acquire new skills to improve their promotion prospects. Mature students often have financial commitments (especially if they are male) and cannot afford to leave jobs to gain new skills. To overcome these problems the government has become involved in retraining. In some areas the retraining is carried out in government skill-centres where the trainee attends for a short concentrated course. Like Justine they receive a weekly wage; it is, however, higher than Justine's allowance and reflects the maturity of their entrants. Some retraining is carried out in colleges under the **Training Opportunities Scheme** (TOPS), especially in the 'service areas'. These include clerical and commercial courses and hotel and catering. In all government retraining there are no fees to trainees.

Marie has been selected for a clerk-typing course at the local college on which she will learn typing and word processing.

Ken

He is now 47 and has been working for the same firm since he was 16 when he joined their apprenticeship scheme. Although his apprenticeship was completed when he was 21 this was not the end of his training. Being a keen and enthusiastic worker he has been promoted, eventually becoming a supervisor.

At this point in his career he discovered that his initial training was insufficient. The skills he learnt as an apprentice were inadequate for a supervisor; he now needed to learn management skills. In many large firms such training would be carried out within the organisation by the training department (usually part of the personnel function) but a small firm may decide to give the employee time off to attend a college or polytechnic. Alternatively Ken may be forced to attend evening classes.

Retraining

The need for retraining so as to acquire new skills is growing because of the development of modern technology (in Ken's case, because of modern management techniques). In the office the typist needs to learn about electronic typewriters and word processors – the accountant and solicitor need to familiarise themselves with computers.

Computer breakthrough

Down on the South Coast a firm of solicitors has set up a link with a computer 4,000 miles away in Dayton, Ohio, giving it access to a huge electronic "library".

Lexis, the legal information service, has 40bn words in its data bank. A further 3m are added each week with reports on criminal tax and industrial law in Britain, the US and France.

It is controlled from Dayton by Mead Data's central mighty computer and in Britain by the law publisher, Butterworth.

Lexis claims to be the world's biggest full-text data retrieval service. "It gives the solicitors far wider access to information at great speed."

The Lexis users in Britain are connected to Dayton via a telephone line. So far, about 5,000 of Britain's 40,000 lawyers use the service. Bosworth is a bit cagey about giving the exact number of law firms on Lexis (he is wary about rivals like Eurolex), but does admit that all the top 12 City firms, all government departments and 50 of the 55 law schools are linked up.

Computerised financial services with information on share prices, currencies and commodities, are growing fast, with firms like Extel, Datasteam and Reuters making the running. Twenty years ago only 40% of Reuters' revenue came from financial services. Now it is 90%, a shift which has revived Reuters' fortunes. Last year it made £36m profit on £179m turnover against 1979's £3m profit on turnover of £76m.

The breakthrough for Reuters came in 1973 with its Monitor service. There are now about 50 separate Monitor services, and 13,000 subscribers using 34,000 terminals in 78 countries.

Reuters' next step is into information processing. Later this year it starts its Data Network, which will offer subscribers a package of sophisticated information to help them deal in the complex world currency markets.

These new skills should be incorporated into training courses for entrants to the professions, while more 'mature' members will need to update theirs.

All the facilities outlined above (colleges, within the firm, etc.) are available for training but the firm selling electronic office equipment will often provide a period of free training for the purchaser's staff. This has the advantage of familiarising the employee with the actual equipment she will be using.

A company runs courses to update staff on new developments and also to improve efficiency within specified areas. In the former category come courses to help staff cope with the changes brought about by Health and Safety regulations or the advent of a new system of sick pay. Improved efficiency would stem from courses in safety (to reduce accidents) or sessions in a supermarket to reduce shoplifting and pilfering; courses in this area can cover a variety of topics as indicated in the following article:

BR turns on the charm

CHARM schools for railwaymen, to encourage diplomacy and good manners in dealing with customers, are being run in Scotland and some parts of England to boost the image of rail travel in the face of severe competition from buses and the airlines.

By the end of the year, 6,000 rail staff who are regularly in contact with the public will have taken a one-day course in Edinburgh or Glasgow which encourages them to seek out customers with problems rather than waiting to be approached. A similar scheme is being tried out in other regions, and the results are being monitored.

The system has already led to a distinct drop in the level of complaints from customers and a measurable increase in passengers in Scotland, although the full effects are not expected to become apparent for some time.

Induction courses

One training course which is common to any job is the **induction course**. This occurs, or should occur, when anybody joins a new organisation whether it be a business or a college. Although it is a form of training it is perhaps more important as a process of welcoming newcomers and making them familiar with their new employer and their new job. As an employee is paid from the first day it is in the firm's interest to get the employee working efficiently as soon as possible. Induction tries to do this, and a guide to systematic induction is set out in Fig. 3.1.

An induction course has three main features.

Fig. 3.1 Sample induction course

> Inductor to initial when covered
> Trainee to initial – instructions received.

Introduction to Co-ops
Structure of P.S.D. Co-op
Departmental structure

Society regulations
Conditions of employment
Wages
Health & safety
Security
Legal requirements
Hygiene – Personal/General
Tour of building

Typing letters
Typing reports
Typing statements
Stencil making & duplication
The filing system
Using the photocopier
Using the word processor

1. The *personal* part of the programme.

This introduces the new employee to colleagues and place of work and deals with company policy. In a college this would involve meeting your new lecturers and being shown around the college. You would see the classrooms, the toilets, the canteen and the library. If there is a students' union you may have a talk from one of the committee. You will be told about college policy on lateness, sickness, fire drills, etc., and finally you will probably be told that if you have any problems at college you should see your course tutor.

In a company the pattern is similar although a different union will be involved and the course tutor is replaced by the personnel department. In addition to company policy on sickness and fire drills the new employee will be informed about holiday entitlement, pension schemes, contracts of employment and payment systems (i.e. methods of calculating pay). Payment systems vary according to the job, and are illustrated by the examples given below.

Andrea
Once she qualifies as an accountant Andrea is likely to be paid a **fixed wage** (salary) regardless of the number of hours she works. It is unlikely that she will be paid overtime. Her wage will be periodically reviewed and as she becomes more experienced it will probably increase. This system is common in the professions and senior management.

Derek
There are various payment systems for manual and blue-collar (skilled) employees. He is paid for **attendance;** this means the union has agreed with the management a basic working week of perhaps 35 hours. A basic hourly rate is agreed (say £3) and each employee receives £105 per week (i.e. 35 x £3). Any hours worked in excess of 35 hours are called overtime and these hours are paid for separately, usually at above the basic rate (e.g. £4 per hour). The hours worked and the basic hourly rate are the subject of annual negotiations with the union.

Evelyn
At the end of her course she obtains employment in a bank. She will be paid on an **incremental system.** This means her wage is fixed but each year it automatically rises by one increment until she reaches the top of the scale.

	Scale A (£)		Scale B (£)
		10	6,400
		9	6,200
		8	6,000
		7	5,800
10	5,600	6	5,600
9	5,400	5	5,400
8	5,200	4	5,200
7	5,000	3	5,000
6	4,800	2	4,800
5	4,600	1	4,600
4	4,400		
3	4,200		
2	4,000		
1	3,800		
0	3,600		

Her starting point on the scale and the scale (A or B) will depend on her age and qualifications but if she remains with the bank long enough she will be paid £5,600 if she is on scale A. She may of course be promoted in which case she would move across onto a higher scale (i.e. B). The scales will be re-adjusted annually because of inflation.

Justine
Although she has finished the YTS course she has been unable to obtain employment in an office and has started work on the production line in a local factory. She is paid by **piece-work.** This means she is paid a fixed amount for each item produced; the more she makes the more she is paid.

Ken
Now he is a supervisor he receives a salary (fixed wage) but he also receives a commission (**payment by results**) which is based on the number of orders his section obtains and processes. The payment-by-result method is commonly used for salesmen and is based on the orders they obtain.

To supplement wages many firms offer 'perks'. These will also be explained to staff. They range from free social club, subsidised canteen through to the company car and expense account.

2. The *company*

To motivate staff you will recall that you should make them feel part of the company. You can start this process on their first day by telling them about the company. This involves its history, its products and perhaps the future. In many organisations new office staff are given a tour around the factory to give them an insight into the company (Wedgewood office staff are sent to Stoke), although this may not occur until they have been with the firm for a certain time.

3. The *job*

This involves telling new employees what is expected of them at work. It may include demonstrations on new machinery and instructions on how the firm wants its letters typed.

Examination questions

1. Many organisations give employees induction training. What do you consider to be the main aspects that should be covered in an induction programme?
   (Q. 12 1977)

2. Explain with an example the difference between 'on-the-job training' and 'off-the-job training'.
   (Q. 1(k) 1975)

3. Explain with examples:
   (*a*) Those aspects of the job of a secretary which can be learned on a college-based course.
   AND
   (*b*) Those which can only be learned from experience at the work place.

   (Q. 4   1980)

4. A Training Officer is anxious to give his new office staff time off each week to attend a local college. The Managing Director says they can learn to do the job and use the equipment under supervision of experienced staff. What points might the Training Officer use to persuade the directors to accept off-the-job training?

   (Q. 6   1982)

Employing staff

Chapter 4

Employing the right staff is important for the employer. She is in business to make a profit and therefore needs efficient staff. She will, of course, train them but this will be much easier if she initially selects staff with the appropriate skills and attitudes.

Engaging staff consists of recruitment, selection, and interviews.

Recruitment

This has a specific meaning and covers the first stages of employing staff. The employer must initially: (a) decide what she wants; (b) attract suitable applicants.

(a) Deciding what she wants

What tasks will she want the new employee to perform? This question is best answered by producing a 'job description' which, as the name suggests, simply describes the job. The format of a job description varies but a typical one might state the title of the job and then describe the major objectives, followed by a more detailed list of the tasks and duties involved in the job. A few examples may help.

Example 1

JOB TITLE   Departmental Assistant to Head of Business Studies.

PURPOSE OF JOB To assist Head in day-to-day running of department.

DUTIES   To type all departmental correspondence.
                 To take minutes at departmental meetings.
                 To keep records of departmental expenditure.
                 To deal with telephone enquiries.
                 To keep departmental records. etc

Example 2

JOB TITLE   Receptionist – School of Chiropody.

PURPOSE OF JOB   To act as receptionist/clerical officer.

DUTIES   The receptionist will be responsible to the Chief Administrative Officer and Head of School.

Reception and booking arrangements within the School.

The issue of appointments to patients and dealing with relevant telephone and personal enquiries together with general assistance to patients.

Collection and receipt of fees for non-priority category patients. Balancing of income and necessary payments to the Finance Office.

Maintenance of patients' records and files – Paramount and Rotadex systems are in operation.

Providing statistical information for internal and external bodies as required.

Input of simple data through a computer terminal.

Example 3

JOB TITLE   Clerk/Typist

Responsibilities and duties
Responsibility will be to the Typing Pool Supervisor.

Duties will include
1. A wide range of audio and copy-typing
2. The use of word-processing equipment
3. Clerical duties

Example 4

JOB TITLE   Junior Secretary
DUTIES

As Example 4 is similar to the type of job you may be applying for, try to complete the above yourself.

Once the job description has been completed then the employer must decide on the personal attributes required of the new staff. I do not smoke; therefore, as I share an office with my secretary, I would require a non-smoker.

Once the employer has compiled the list, then he or she should draw up a chart listing the qualities required under two headings, 'Essential' and 'Desirable'.

Again let us consider some examples.

Example 5

JOB TITLE   Departmental Assistant

QUALITY	ESSENTIAL	DESIRABLE
Type	RSA 111 typing	RSA 11 audio
Keep minutes	80 wpm shorthand	
Skill with figures	Numerate	'O' level Maths or CSE 1
Telephone manner	Well spoken	
Keeping records	Organisational skill	Experience in a secretarial capacity
	Non-smoker	
	Smart appearance	
	Good time keeper	
	Work without supervision	
	etc	

Example 6

JOB TITLE   Receptionist

QUALITY	ESSENTIAL	DESIRABLE
Reception	Smart and well spoken	
Booking arrangements	Efficient organiser	
Assisting patients	Sympathetic manner	
Collection of fees	Numerate	CSE 2 or above in Maths
Input of data	Ability to use a keyboard	RSA 1 typing
		Experience of computer
	etc	

Example 7

JOB TITLE   Junior Secretarial

QUALITY	ESSENTIAL	DESIRABLE

What qualities do you think your future employer will be looking for at your interview? Write them in on Example 7 and then ask yourself what you need to do to acquire them.

(b) Attracting suitable applicants

This means bringing the vacancy to the attention of suitably qualified people. They may already exist within your organisation waiting to be promoted. They can be notified through an internal newsletter or on staff notice boards.

Most appointments are, however, made from outside the company. If a firm is seeking a junior secretary it may not advertise the post, preferring to use contacts in either the local College of Further Education or the Careers Service. The former is frequently used because, apart from being free, the college is likely to send along only suitable applicants, whereas anybody can reply to an advertisement.

Where the employer requires an experienced secretary, then the College or the Careers Service would be inappropriate and the Job Centre or a private agency might be used instead. The latter is very expensive.

The most common method of publicising a vacancy is, however, the newspaper advertisement, either in the local or national press. If we restrict our discussions to office staff then a national advertisement is unnecessary as we would expect to attract sufficient suitably qualified applicants from our locality. In order to obtain a suitable response from the advertisement (i.e. getting people to apply) the employer must ensure that the advertisement's content is right and that it appears at the right time (i.e. when the prospective employee is likely to read the paper.)

A suitable advertisement should provide sufficient information to enable the reader to decide if they want to apply, e.g.

- details of company and location of job
- details of job
- qualifications required
- salary payable (this is often omitted, especially where it is low!)
- procedure for applying.

Once the advertisement is drafted then the type of advertisement must be decided. Should it be classified or displayed? (See Fig. 4.1)

Fig. 4.1

CLASSIFIED

SOLICITORS require an Operator for a Word Processor. Training will be provided but previous experience an advantage. Applicants must have legal experience preferably in Conveyancing. 4 weeks annual holiday. Salary according to experience. – Apply in writing to ...

JUNIOR Clerk Typist required for general office duties. Typing essential. 37½-hour week to include Saturday morning. Preferred resident in Plympton area. – Apply in writing only with details of age and qualifications to: ......

AUDIO Typist required for busy Plymouth Estate Agents. Must have experience with electric machines. Most demanding and responsible position. – Apply Box No. ....

DARTINGTON. Secretary, salary to £5,200 p.a. There is a vacancy for a full time secretary to the Department of Art and Design at Dartington College of Arts. The work includes acting as secretary to the Head of Department and doing administrative and typing work for the rest of the department. – Letter of application with CV by 25th March to the Senior Administrative Officer, ...

SECRETARY required for Powderham Estate Office, some experience, audio typing. Accommodation available. – Apply in writing with c.v., to ......

WANTED Audio Secretary for Solicitors, North Hill area, conveyancing experience essential, salary £3,300, possible flexibility of hours. – Telephone Plymouth ....

DISPLAY

SECRETARIAL APPOINTMENT

Local branch office of leading Life Assurance Company requires Shorthand Typist. Pleasant working environment, five day week, luncheon vouchers, salary from £3,576, dependent upon age and qualifications. Position would ideally suit applicants in age range of 18 to 25 with proficient shorthand and typing abilities.

Please telephone or write to ....

....

....

COLLEGE OF
ST. MARK & ST JOHN
PLYMOUTH
SECRETARY/ CLERICAL ASSISTANT

for a very busy office. Salary A.P.T. plus C. (£4,014, under review). Annual contract for the Mode A Youth Training Programme, capable of supporting a hard-working team. Good secretarial skills required. Letters of application and curriculum vitae to:

P.A./SECRETARY
to Company Secretary.

A vacancy exists for an agile minded accounts office experienced person of 21 years or more with abilities in shorthand and typing to assist the Company Director in his administrative and financial roles. Starting salary £3,750 p.a.

Applications in writing with full c.v. to:

VIDEO PA/ SECRETARY

Longman Video's small marketing team need PA with plenty of initiative and flexibility. Good secretarial and organisational skills to handle customer relations involvement in marketing activity and sales admin systems. Salary range £5,500 – £6,700 plus £1 per day L.V's.

Tel:...............................

SECRETARY P.A. c£7,000

For the senior partner of a small firm of Computer Consultants with responsibility for personnel and some administration. Speeds 90/50wpm, willingness to learn W.P. Ability to organise essential – scope for great involvement in an expanding company.

For further details please contact:

Having made that decision the day or days of the week on which it will be inserted must be agreed. Friday evening seems to be a favoured time.

Selection

This covers the remaining stages in engaging staff. The application procedure specified in the advertisement may have included providing a curriculum vitae (c.v.) with a letter of application or the completion of an application form to be returned to the prospective employer. A short list of suitable candidates can then be prepared based on the information supplied. The curriculum vitae can be particularly important as it may provide additional information not covered by a letter of application or an application form. It might help to secure an interview. (Two c.v.'s produced by SSC students can be found in Figs 4.2 and 4.3).

The application forms and c.v.s are then assessed and compared against the essential and desirable characteristics chart. Anybody lacking the former will not be short-listed; assuming there is still a choice, the best three to six will be short-listed and invited for interview.

The final selection can be by interview or by interview and test. For a secretarial position the test might consist of a dictation exercise with a typed transcript. With most posts the interviewer will, however, accept external examination certificates as proof of competence and so the job selection depends on the interview.

Interview

The student about to apply for her first post needs to know something about the interview process because this knowledge may help to avoid some of the pitfalls and give her an advantage over the other applicants.

No matter how competent you are, you will not obtain employment unless you impress at an interview. Your interview performance must improve if you know what the interviewer is looking for, as this helps you give the right answers!

What therefore does the interviewer look for? She begins by checking the information on your application and then seeks to assess your suitability for the post. She will do this by asking questions. When asking these she should follow certain rules; these include:
1. Don't ask questions that can be answered YES/NO. This type of question will not provide much information about the candidate.

Fig. 4.2 Example of a c.v.

Curriculum vitae

SURNAME	Cooper
FORENAME(S)	Sheila
ADDRESS	Southway, Plymouth, Devon
DATE OF BIRTH	23 March 1966 AGE: 17
STATUS	Single
SCHOOLS	Plymstock Comprehensive (1977–78) Crownhill Secondary Modern (1978–82) College of Further Education (1982–83)

EDUCATIONAL QUALIFICATIONS

English Language	GCE B
English Literature	GCE C
Biology	CSE 1
History	CSE 2
Mathematics	CSE 4
French	CSE 4

VOCATIONAL QUALIFICATIONS EXPECTED

Shorthand	LCC 70/80
Typing	RSA II, III
	LCC Intermediate
	LCC Higher
	LCC Certificate in Secretarial studies
English Language	RSA II
Audio Typing	RSA II
Oral Communications	ESB (Elementary)

HOBBIES AND INTERESTS

Disco dancing, reading, swimming, going to discos, travelling, jogging, listening to records and learning to drive, meeting people and walking.

REFEREES

Mr A. R. Leal **Head of Business Studies** College of Further Education Paradise Road Devonport	Ms. B. Jones 56 Rushfield Sawbridgeworth Herts

Fig. 4.2 Example of a c.v.

Curriculum vitae

SURNAME   Holt

FORENAME(S)   Jennifer

ADDRESS   Southway, Plymouth, Devon

DATE OF BIRTH   9 February 1966   AGE: 17

STATUS   Single

SCHOOLS   Plympton Secondary (1977–1982)
                   College of Further Education (1982–83)

EDUCATIONAL QUALIFICATIONS

English Language	O Level B
English Language	CSE 1
English Literature	CSE 2
Geography	CSE 1
Rural Science	CSE 1
History	CSE 1

VOCATIONAL QUALIFICATIONS

Typewriting	CSE 2

VOCATIONAL QUALIFICATIONS EXPECTED

Shorthand	LCC 90/100
	LCC 70/80
	RSA 80
Typewriting	RSA II
	LCC Intermediate
	LCC Higher
	LCC Certificate in Secretarial Studies
English Language	RSA I
Audio Typing	RSA II
Oral Communications	ESB (Elementary)

HOBBIES AND INTERESTS

Gliding, swimming, badminton, roller skating, music, playing the guitar.

PREVIOUS EXPERIENCE

Working in secretary's office at a Primary School.

REFEREES

Mr A. R. Leal
Head of Business Studies
College of Further Education
Paradise Road
DEVONPORT

Miss A. Smith
Dene House
Lower Road
Lichfield
Staffs.

2. Don't lead the candidate by 'suggesting' the appropriate answer in the question. (What would be your answer to the question, 'I believe in punctuality don't you?')
3. Do ask follow-up questions. This means that answers should be probed. The interviewer might ask, 'What sort of experience have you had?' The reply might be, 'As a secretary to an estate agent.' This does not provide much information to the interviewer so she must probe further by asking, 'What did your duties involve as secretary?'

As the person being interviewed what rules should you follow? First, remember you are trying to show the employer you possess the qualities she is looking for. You should know what these are (you listed them for a junior secretarial post in Example 7). At the interview you must 'get these qualities across'.

Many of the personal qualities can be illustrated before the interview. Turn up early, dress smartly and don't chew gum! At the actual interview it is up to you to prove you are right for the job. A good interviewer will help by asking the right questions but the onus is always on you to present your case. Suppose an interviewer asked, 'Do you want this job?' Admittedly it is a poor question because you can answer Yes. Don't! Use the answer to give the interviewer information you feel will help your case. You might reply, 'Yes because I know this is a good company to work for. I discussed it with my Course Tutor at college . . .' Your answer now tells the interviewer you have thought about the job. A plus for you.

You may have taken part in the Duke of Edinburgh scheme. Try to get this information across because it will impress. The interviewer may ask you if you have a Saturday job. You might not have worked on Saturday. Rather than simply tell her that, you can continue by pointing out that your weekends were involved doing the scheme. You have again scored a plus.

To summarise. A good interviewee works out what the interviewer will be looking for. She decides what information to give and at the interview tries to pass on as much of this information as she can.*

At the end of the interview the candidate leaves and the interviewer should make written notes about her performance. This should be done before the next candidate arrives. At the end of the interviews these notes will help to ensure that the best candidate is appointed.

References are usually obtained before the interview but must be treated with scepticism. They are often only another person's view of the candidate and may therefore be biased; a reference should be a guide to the interviewer and should not be the sole criteria for selection.

* More information on interviews is included on the cassette tape which accompanies this book.

Sources of consumer finance

Chapter 5

On your first day at work you will normally attend an induction course. During it you are informed that the firm will arrange for your wages to be paid directly into your bank account. This is advantageous for the firm because:

1. *It is secure*: the transactions are made by a computer which transfers money from the firm's account into yours. This removes the need to transfer large sums of money from the bank to the firm, and hence avoids the necessity of hiring a security firm to transfer it.
2. *It is cheaper*: Apart from the 'security' aspect savings are also made in staffing. The firm no longer has to employ staff to make up wage packets, i.e. put the correct amount of cash into each packet.
3. *The firm's cash remains in the bank longer*: Money can earn interest in a bank. If the firm has to make up wage packets then it must withdraw money on Wednesday if it is to have wage packets ready on Friday. Paying directly into your account means the money is transferred out of the firm's account on Friday; the firm obtains two more days' interest each time wages are paid. In a large firm with a substantial wage bill the interest earned can be considerable.

Imagine that to explain the advantages to the staff the firm have invited the local bank manager to answer questions.

Q. *If my wages are paid directly into my account how do I get cash?*
A. The money is paid into what we call a **current account.** Once this is opened you are given a cheque book. If you want to draw out money you write out a cheque, bring it into the bank and my staff will give you cash for it.
Q. *But I work Monday to Friday and can't get into a bank.*
A. Don't worry, we've thought of that. You will also be issued with a cash card [an example is shown in Fig. 5.1.]; this enables you to draw cash from a point outside the bank (called a 'cash dispenser') at any time, including evenings and weekends. All you do is put in the card, key in your personal code number (which only you know) and the

Fig. 5.1

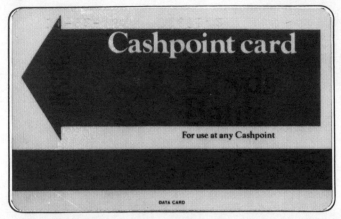

amount you want and the cash will be delivered to you. I don't recommend you carry large sums of cash because of the spate of bag snatching. Just use your cheque book to buy things, only use cash for small items like bus fares.

Fig. 5.2

Q. *Won't some businesses refuse to accept cheques?*
A. This used to be a problem because shops couldn't be sure that you had enough money in your account to cover the cheque. We've solved that by issuing our customers with a **cheque card** [see Fig. 5.2]. This guarantees payment of any cheque you write providing it is for less than £50. The bank will honour (that is pay) the cheque even if you have no funds in your account; you will, of course, have to repay the bank and if you keep over-drawing your account we may withdraw the card.
Q. *This sounds all very well but what's it going to cost me?*
A. That's a good question. It does cost the bank a lot of money to handle cheques but providing you keep a minimum of £100 in your

current account we will provide all services free.

Q. *That seems a lot of money.*

A. Not really, because apart from cheque books there are other services that are available to you. I mentioned earlier that you could pay your bills by cheque. The bank has a system called a **'standing order'** which enables us to pay regular bills for you without you having to remind us. If you have an annual subscription to a club or a monthly payment for rates, rent, mortgage etc all you have to do is to inform the bank when the payments are due and how much. We will automatically transfer the amount from your account to the other party. You don't have to do anything.

Q. *Won't I have to tell you if the amount changes?*

A. Yes. This is why we recommend standing orders for regular payments of fixed sums. If you pay different sums at fixed intervals then I suggest you use a **direct debit**. This enables the people to whom you owe money to contact the bank and tell us how much you owe them. The bank will then automatically transfer this sum from your account to theirs.

Q. *How do I know you're not paying them too much?*

A. Occasionally, monthly if you like, the bank will send you a bank statement [see Fig. 5.3] which lists all the transactions on your

Fig. 5.3

| ACCOUNT NUMBER | | In account with | SHEET 5 | |
| ACCOUNT HOLDERS NAME | | **National Westminster Bank PLC** | | |

1983			PLYMSTOCK BRANCH	
Date	Details	Debits	Credits	Balance
14APR	Balance Forward			100.00
15APR	000061	106.20		
	.REV AUTO TRF	74.59		
	AUTOMATIC TRANSFER TR		180.79	100.00
18APR	.REV AUTO TF	180.79		80.79 %
21APR	MBIS INSURANCE PRM DD	2.50		83.29 %
25APR	D.C.C. SALARIES -		1,250.38	1,167.09
26APR	000065	5.90		
	STANDARD LIFE A CO DD	35.10		1,126.09
27APR	000063	121.13		
	000069	35.00		
	CASH/CHEQUES		97.50	1,067.46
28APR	000066	20.00		
	000067	12.23		
	000071	267.00		768.23
29APR	.CASH/CHEQUES		124.07	892.30
3MAY	000072	17.65		
	HALIFAX B/S SO	149.24		
	PLYMOUTH CITY CNCL SO	52.26		673.15
4MAY	000068	18.24		
	000070	3.70		651.21
6MAY	000064	3.00		
	000073	15.00		
	CASH/CHEQUES		5.00	638.21
9MAY	000075	15.00		623.21
13MAY	LONGMAN ROYALTIES -		996.71	1,619.92
16MAY	000077	17.85		1,602.07
18MAY	000074	13.47		
	000076	9.92		1,578.68
23MAY	MBIS INSURANCE PRM DD	2.50		1,576.18
24MAY	NORWICH UNION LIFE DD	21.25		1,554.93

| Abbreviations | CD Cash Dispensed | DV Dividend | TR Transfer | O D indicates an |
| | DD Direct Debit | SO Standing Order | | Overdrawn Balance |

account. You can check all the transactions (both in and out) and if you're not satisfied just come into the bank and we will check them for you.

Q. *Can I pay several bills with one cheque?*

A. Yes. You use a **credit transfer.** One cheque is written for the whole amount with instructions as to its division among your various creditors. The bank will then arrange for them to be paid.

Q. *That seems good value for £100. If I have more than £100 in my account do I get interest?*

A. We're looking into that and it may be possible in the future but at present we do not pay interest on current accounts. What I suggest is that you open a **deposit account.** We will pay you interest on this but you can't write cheques on it. If you want to withdraw money from this account we will require notice although if it's for small sums we will waive the notice. What we can do is to transfer automatically part of your salary into the deposit account each month. As a bonus if your current account ever falls below £100 we can arrange for an automatic transfer from your deposit account. This way you'll never pay bank charges

Q. *We've just been told by personnel that we get paid at the end of each month. How am I to live until I receive my first month's salary?*

A. The bank appreciates that you may have cash problems when you start work so we'll give you **overdraft** facilities.

Q. *What's that?*

A. Basically it means we will let you write cheques up to a certain amount on your current account when it has no money in it. We will, of course, have to charge interest on the sum overdrawn and you will have to repay it over a certain period.

Q. *I'm not sure I understand. Could you give me an example?*

A. Certainly. Suppose your account has £100 in it. You want to buy items which will cost £200. We will let you have overdraft facilities of £100. Now you can write out a cheque for £200. You owe us £100 which you must pay back in 10 monthly instalments of £10. You pay interest on £100 for the first month, on £90 for the second, on £80 for the third and so on.

There are no more questions and the talk ends.

Budget accounts

As you are starting work you decide the clothes you wore at college are no longer suitable. You need smarter ones. You could use your overdraft facility but you will have to pay interest. Instead you decide to buy your clothes at a local store where they advertise 'budget accounts'.

When you enter the store you visit the Accounts department who explain how the system works. You agree to pay a fixed monthly sum regardless of purchases. Once you have paid the first sum this means that you can automatically spend 24 times this amount. Thus if you agree to pay £10 you can automatically purchase £240 worth of clothes. If you spend £240 this means your credit is exhausted but it will rise by £10 each month (the sum you pay) minus, of course, any other purchases you make. (See table 5.1.)

Table 5.1.

Month	Payment	Purchases	Outstanding credit
1	10	220	20
2	10	—	30
3	10	—	40
4	10	—	50
5	10	—	40
6	10	—	*
7	10	—	*
8	10	30	*

fill in the blank figures

After several years at work you get married and decide to purchase a house. Banks do give loans to purchase property but the rate of interest they charge is often higher than building societies (you can check on the current situation by contacting your bank and building society). As the building society rate is lower you decide to apply to them for a mortgage.

Building societies

Building societies lend money but for one purpose only; the purchase of property or its improvement. That operation falls into two parts.

1. Raising money

Individuals or institutions (such as pension funds) have surplus cash on which they want to earn interest. They can safely invest it in various ways, e.g.:

- Deposit accounts at banks
- Gilt-edge securities
- Building society accounts

The choice of investment is primarily determined by the rate of interest. You will invest your funds where they will obtain the highest return (providing the risk is acceptable). The banks and building societies (and to a lesser extent the government) are in competition for your money and each seeks to persuade you that they offer the best terms.

This competition for funds naturally benefits the investor and has led to a wide range of schemes being offered. The building societies offer an account which combines the advantages of both the current and deposit accounts of the bank. You can write cheques on it; money can be withdrawn immediately (unless the sum is very large, then a short period of notice is required) and it gains interest though at the lowest of the rates offered by the society. Additionally the societies have sought to make their facilities more attractive by opening on Saturdays and issuing cash cards.

You will recall that not all these facilities are available to holders of deposit accounts at banks, nor do all banks open on Saturday. However, some banks have retaliated. At least one is experimenting with Saturday morning opening, and some are considering paying interest on current accounts. This whole area is changing rapidly and students are advised to watch for developments; an easy way of doing this is to watch television adverts, as both banks and building societies use this medium to advise the public of their services.

The building societies have also tried to attract funds by offering additional interest to investors who are prepared to leave their cash in the societies for a minimum period (this competes with the government's national savings scheme). The schemes offered by all the societies are so numerous (and often complicated) that one society simplified its schemes and promoted them with the slogan 'find your way through the money maze by . . .'. As with the above this is an area of rapid change and students are advised to visit a couple of their local societies to gather leaflets on the schemes available. You will then be capable of answering topical questions.

You will probably find that the accounts offered to investors fall into three main categories.

(a) *Paid-up share accounts* (this is their equivalent to the deposit accounts). The rate of interest at the time of writing is 6¼ per cent.

(b) *A regular investment account.* A higher rate of interest is offered if you agree to deposit a fixed sum each month for a set period. The societies like this type of account because once you have committed yourself you cannot withdraw the funds if you discover there is a better rate of interest available elsewhere. The interest rate at the time of writing is 7¼ per cent.

(c) If you invest a lump sum (there is usually a minimum figure) and agree to leave it in the society for a fixed period this also achieves a high rate of interest. If you withdraw it before the agreed time you usually lose part of the interest. The rate of interest at the time of writing is 7½ per cent.

You have probably realised that when building societies fix the interest rates payable to investors they must take into account the interest available at, for example, banks. If building societies rates are lower than those operating elsewhere then fewer people will invest with them. Conversely, as we will see in a moment, the interest rates

payable by borrowers are determined by the rates paid to investors. It
follows that the lower the rates paid to investors the lower the
rates borrowers will have to pay. The societies therefore attempt to set
rates at which the money investors pay in equals the amount customers
want to borrow.

Example
Rate to investors 10 per cent: amount invested £100 m.
Rate to borrowers 13 per cent: amount borrowed £140 m.
  The building societies cannot satisfy all potential borrowers, they are £40 m. short.
Therefore:
Rate to investors 10½ per cent: amount invested £120 m.
Rate to borrowers 13½ per cent: amount borrowed £120 m.

The additional ½ per cent paid to investors has increased the inflow
of funds (investors now find it more profitable at building societies)
while the additional ½ per cent has discouraged a number of potential
borrowers. If, therefore, the inflow of funds falls in any month (and
this figure is reported in the press) there could be a 'mortgage famine'
or 'mortgage queue'. If you see this type of headline in a newspaper it
could mean a rise in mortgage rates to enable a higher rate to be paid to
investors.

All interest rates may rise or fall as a result of government policy for
reasons which are explained elsewhere.

2. Lending money

When building societies lend money to enable the purchase of
property they are said to be granting a **mortgage.** A prospective
borrower (who is called the mortgagee once she receives the loan) will
approach a building society with a request for a mortgage. If the
society has sufficient funds it will ask her to fill in a mortgage
application form (Fig. 5.4). (If there is a shortage of funds a building
society will 'ration' mortgages and probably give priority to its own
investors; this is a good reason for saving with a society.)

The amount of the mortgage depends on two factors. The first is the
income of the applicant (and if married, the spouse). The society has a
responsibility to its investors (whose money they are lending) to lend
sensibly and it must therefore try to ensure morgagees have sufficient
income to be able to repay the loan. For this reason societies usually
only lend 2½ to 3 times the income of the applicant.

Example
Income £10,000: max loan £25,000–£30,000.
Income £15,000: max loan £37,500–£45,000.

The second factor is the value of the property. As stated above, the
society is responsible for safeguarding investors' funds and so it must
guard against the possibility that the mortgagee will not be able to
repay the loan (i.e. **default**). This might arise because of redundancy or
possibly death. The mortgage is therefore 'secured' on the property.

CONFIDENTIAL

FULL NAME (PLEASE USE BLOCK CAPITALS)

Title   Surname

Forenames

Married or Single _____   Date of Birth _____

Number of dependent children _____   Their ages _____

PRESENT RESIDENCE

Address

Town

County   Post Code

If this is rented accommodation please give details of the rent paid per week. £ _____

If the property is mortgaged please give the account or roll number. _____

    Please give the name and address of your Landlord or Mortgagee (Lender).

If you are not a Tenant or Mortgagor please give details.

If your present residence is not in mortgage have you or your spouse had a mortgage on any property during the last

five years? _____ If so please give details. _____

INVESTMENTS

If you have any investments with the Society please give the account numbers.

BANKRUPTCY

Have you ever been bankrupt or entered into any arrangement with creditors or is there any judgement for debt

outstanding? _____

If so please give details. _____

EMPLOYMENT - EMPLOYEE

If you are an employee please give the name and address of your employer.

_____

_____

_____

Your present position there. _____

Annual income:-

        Basic earnings.   £ _____

        Overtime.   £ _____

        Bonus.   £ _____

        Commission.   £ _____

        Total.   £ _____

How long have you been in your present employment? _____

The Society will normally require confirmation of the above details from your employer. Please therefore state:-

    The Department to which reference should be made (if applicable). _____

    The Name and position of the person to whom reference should be made (if known).

    _____

    Your Works or Staff Number (if applicable). _____

Please state the amount of any additional income apart from that shown above £ _____ per year.

    From what source is it derived? _____

EMPLOYMENT - SELF EMPLOYED

If you are self employed please state the nature of your business.

_____

Name and address of your business. _____

_____

Name and address of your accountants. _____

_____

How long has the business been established? _____

Your **annual** income derived from it. £ _____

Please supply copies of audited accounts for the last three years or failing these, income tax assessments for the same period.

Please state the amount of any additional income apart from that shown above £ _____ per year.

    From what source is it derived? _____

Please state the name and address of your bank. _____

_____ Account No. |__|__|__|__|__|__|__|__|

AUTHORITY

I authorise the Society to refer to my Accountants/Employer/Landlord/Mortgagee/Bankers if necessary.

I agree to the information on this form being supplied to the Insurance Company/Local Authority if at my request the Society makes application for a guarantee with this loan.

Signed _____ Date _____

APPLICATION FOR LOAN

Please give the information in the spaces provided or tick the appropriate box. ☑
Please use BLOCK CAPITALS.

A   THE APPLICANTS

	(Forenames)	(Surname)
010		
011		
012		
013		

Note: The names written here must be identical with the names of the purchaser(s) of the property, e.g. if the property is held or
is to be held in the joint names of husband and wife, both names should be given.

B   THE PROPERTY

Full Postal Address of the Property.

100	
101	
102	Town
103	County Post Code

1   DESCRIPTION

		House	Bungalow	Converted Flat or Maisonette	Purpose Built Flat or Maisonette	Other
Tick the kind of property. ➤	104	0	1	2	3	4

If OTHER please give details.

		Semi-Detached	Detached	Terraced	Other
Is the Property ➤	105	0	1	2	3

If a FLAT or MAISONETTE
How many storeys are there in the block? ➤ | 106 |

		Yes	No
Are there any business premises in the block? ➤	107	1	0

If YES please give details.

If the flat is subject to an annual service charge, please show the current amount payable. ➤ £

2   GARAGE

	Yes	No
Is a garage included? ➤		

2

3 **AREA OF LAND**

Is a garden included? . . . . ► 108

	Yes		No	
108	0		1	

If there is more than one acre of land, please state how much land. . . . . . ► 109

109		Acres

4 **NEW PROPERTY**

If the property is new please give the name and address of the builder.

Is the builder registered with the National House Builders' Council? . . ► 110

	Yes		No	
110	1		0	

5 **ROAD CHARGES**

Have the roads adjoining the property been taken over by the appropriate Authorities? . . ►

Yes	No

Have the sewers used by the property been taken over by the appropriate Authorities? . . ►

Yes	No

6 **TENURE**

Indicate the tenure of the property. . . . . ► 115

	Freehold		Leasehold		Feudal	
115	0		1		2	

If FREEHOLD please state amount of any Chief Rent or if FEUDAL amount of any Feu Duty.

116	£	

If LEASEHOLD please state the term of years. . . . . ► 117

117		years

The term of years starts from (state year only). . . . . ► 118

118	

Amount of the Ground Rent. . . . . ► 119

119	£	

Can the Ground Rent be increased? . . . . ► 120

	Yes		No	
120	1		0	

If YES please state how often and give the amount.

7 **OWNERSHIP**

Do you already own the property? . . . . ► 125

	Yes		No	
125	1		0	

If you have a mortgage on the property, please state the present debt, the name of the mortgagee (lender) and the reason for wishing to repay that mortgage.

Do you intend to purchase the property under a shared ownership scheme or do you already own the property under such a scheme? . . . . . . ► 126

	Yes		No	
126	1		0	

8 **VENDOR**

Please indicate if you are buying from one of the following:- . . . . ► 128

	Local Authority		New Town Corporation		Housing Association		National Coal Board	
128	1		2		3		4	

3

9 OCCUPATION OF THE PROPERTY

Do you occupy the property now? · · · · · · · · · · · · · ►

	Yes		No	
130	1		0	

Will you be given full vacant possession of all the property on completion of your purchase? · ►

Yes	No

Will you occupy the property as soon as you complete your purchase? · · · · · · · ►

Yes	No

How much of the property will you occupy? · · · · · · · ►

	Whole		Part		None	
131	0		1		2	

Will any persons who are aged seventeen or more but will not be parties to the mortgage live at the property with you? · · · · · · · · · · · ►

Yes	No

If YES please give their full names (and present address if different from your address). They will have to allow the Society's mortgage to come before their interest in the property.

_____

_____

_____

_____

10 INSPECTION BY THE VALUER

If the property is now occupied please give the name and telephone number of the occupier.

_____

_____

If the property is unoccupied where can the key be obtained? _____

_____

11 ESTATE AGENTS

Name and address of estate agents (if any) through whom you are purchasing.

_____

_____

12 PURCHASE PRICE

Amount of Purchase Price. · · · · · · · · · · · · · · · · ► £

Where any carpets, curtains etc. worth more than £2,000 are included, state their value. · · ► £

Net Price (after deducting the above stated value of carpets, etc.). · · · · · · ► 135 £

Add cost of any improvements or alterations you intend to make. · · · · · ► 136 £

Total £

13 LOCAL AUTHORITY GRANT

If you are obtaining a grant from the Local Authority please state how much. · · · ► 137 £

C THE LOAN 4

Please state the amount of loan you require. ► | **200** | £ |

Period of Repayment you prefer. ► | **201** | | years |

	Yes	No

If the property is being built will part of the loan be needed during building? ►

	Yes	No

Do you intend to apply for assistance under the Home Purchase Assistance Scheme? ►

	Yes	No

Do you require an Option Mortgage? ► | **203** | 1 | 0 |

If YES please state countries of residence during the last 5 years if outside the United Kingdom.

Are you finding out of your own money the full difference between the amount of the loan and the total cost of the property? ►

	Yes	No

If NO state who is providing the balance of the money and the amount.

1 METHOD OF REPAYMENT

The loan may be repaid by a monthly standing order from an investment account with the Society, a monthly standing order from your bank account, or payment at any of the Society's branches.

Please indicate your preference. ► | **204** | | |

HBS Standing Order	Bank Standing Order	Payment at Branch
1	0	2

2 LIFE ASSURANCE

The Society recommends that to protect your dependants, you should arrange life assurance to cover the loan. The Society can arrange life assurance and advise you about different kinds of policies.

Alternatively would you prefer a representative from an insurance company to call to see you? ►

	Yes	No

Kind of life assurance required (if known) ►

ENDOWMENT		MORTGAGE PROTECTION	
Full	Low Cost	Convertible Term Assurance	Decreasing Term Assurance

Do you already have an endowment policy or policies which you wish to use. ►

	Yes	No

If YES please give details of the policies.

Policy Number	Company Name	Sum Assured

D CORRESPONDENCE ADDRESS

Please give the address to which letters may be sent before completion of the purchase.

501	
502	
503	Town
504	County Post Code

If you can be contacted by telephone please state the number.

5

E   PROPERTY INSURANCE

The Society's Valuer will estimate the sum needed to rebuild the property in the same form if it is destroyed. The property will be insured for this amount. To allow for rising costs the insurance value will be adjusted monthly in line with the 'House Rebuilding Cost Index' which is prepared by the Royal Institution of Chartered Surveyors or some similar index. The premium will be amended yearly and it is likely to increase each year.

PURCHASERS OF PROPERTY ARE NORMALLY LIABLE FOR ALL RISKS FROM THE DATE OF THE EXCHANGE OF CONTRACTS TO PURCHASE

In the case of a private dwelling the Society will arrange a houseowner's insurance on the property when the cheque for the loan is sent unless insurance cover has been requested from an earlier date. Special arrangements will be made for other types of property where houseowner's insurance is not available. Your account will be charged with the premiums.

If you would like other insurance arrangements to be considered please give details_____

Of what materials are the walls and roof made? _____

If any business is to be carried out at the property please give details. _____

F   SOLICITORS

Please give the name and address of your Solicitors.

Name or reference of the person dealing with your purchase. · · · · · · · · · · · ► | 706 |

G   DECLARATION

I apply for a loan on the security of the property described in this application and declare that I am over 18 and believe that the information given in this application is correct. I accept that

1) the payment of the valuation fee shall not bind the Society to grant an advance,
2) the Society does not warrant that the purchase price of the property is reasonable,
3) the valuation obtained by the Society is solely for its own use in deciding how much to lend, and
4) the Valuer will make a limited inspection of the property which will not be as extensive as a survey.

The Society will provide you with a copy of its report and valuation but YOU ARE RECOMMENDED TO ARRANGE A MORE DETAILED INSPECTION FOR YOUR OWN PROTECTION. The Society's Valuer may be willing to do this for you for an extra fee.

Would you like to have a House Buyers Inspection Report? THIS WILL BE SUBJECT TO STANDARD PUBLISHED CONDITIONS OR TERMS OF ENGAGEMENT WHICH ARE AVAILABLE ON REQUEST. · · · · · · · · · · · · · · · · · · ► | Yes | No |

Would you like to have a separate survey by the Society's Valuer? · · · · · · · · · ► | Yes | No |

Applicant's usual signature _____ Age _____

Date _____

6

Valuation Fee Paid. · ► £ _____

Administration and Indemnity Fee Paid. · · · · · · · · · · · · · ► £ _____

Date Valuation Fee Paid. · · · · · · · · · · · · · · · · · · ► _____

Source of Introduction. _____

Branch	Agency
BRANCH RECOMMENDATION	AGENT'S RECOMMENDATION
Signature of Interviewer Date	
Recommended by: Date	Signature Date
Signature	
Designation	

Form 1/50004-8 (12/82)

In the event of default the society can sell the house, recoup the amount of the mortgage and hand over any surplus from the sale to the mortgagee. Obviously, then, the society will not lend more than the value of the house. In determining a house's value a society will take a pessimistic view; it is valued at the lowest price a society could get assuming there was a slump in the housing market. Thus you might buy a new house for £30,000 but find that a society values it at only £28,000. The valuation is made by a surveyor employed by the society but the prospective borrower must pay the surveyor's fee!

After the house has been valued the society will, if satisfied, offer you a mortgage. This will be for a period of up to 25 years (although sometimes it will be longer) and you will repay it monthly. Normally you would use a standing order on your current account. The value of the standing order may need to be changed periodically because if interest rates alter the amount of your monthly repayments will also change.

You have accepted the mortgage offer. All that remains is to finalise the purchase of the house. Your solicitor will ensure that all the legal formalities are complied with; the final step is to hand over the purchase price in return for the deeds of the property (these prove you are the legal owner). At this point you have a problem! The sellers of the house will not hand over the deeds if you give them a cheque because it takes several days for a cheque to clear. If they give you the deeds and the bank refuses to honour your cheque (because there are insufficient funds in your account) the house sellers have a problem. The building society will not, however, hand over the mortgage money until they receive the deeds because this is their **collateral** for the mortgage. The problem could be solved if you paid cash but this is risky because of the possibility of theft. A much more sensible approach would be to use a **'bank draft'**. This is a cheque which is drawn on the bank. The house purchaser may be paying £3,000 with the building society paying £24,000. The purchaser gives her bank a cheque for £3,000; they debit her account and give her a bank draft for £3,000. This states that the bank will pay the seller (this name would be on the draft) £3,000. The latter knows the bank has the money to honour the cheque so it will be accepted; the draft is as good as cash but as it can only be cashed by the person named. It is secure. The drafts from the purchaser and building society are handed over and the deeds are given to the building society.

The transaction can now take place and you will become a house owner.

Credit finance

Very soon you will want to purchase items for your house. Some of these (television, washing machine, refrigerator) are expensive. You can wait until you have saved enough money before purchasing them but you may consider buying them on credit.

One method of obtaining credit is to approach your bank manager for a **loan.** This is different from an overdraft in that you borrow a fixed sum of money to spend on a specified item or items (with an overdraft you can spend it how you like). You will have to persuade your bank manager that the expenditure is 'sensible' and prove that you can repay the loan. To cover the possibility of you defaulting (being unable to pay) he will probably ask you to provide either collateral (security) or a guarantor for the loan. If you default then the collateral will be sold or the guarantor will have to repay the sum borrowed on your behalf. As with an overdraft you have to pay interest until the loan is repaid.

An alternative is to purchase the goods on **hire purchase.** The item is purchased from the retailer but instead of paying the full purchase price you only pay a deposit (perhaps 10 per cent of the price). The remainder (90%) plus interest is paid off in monthly instalments over a fixed period. Once the last instalment has been paid the goods become your property; if you fail to pay any instalments the retailer can ask the court for permission to repossess the goods. This may be granted or the court may give you time to pay off the arrears.

Fig. 5.5

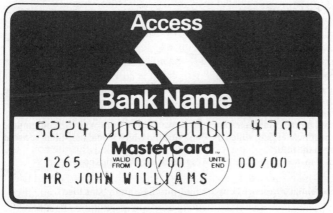

If you have the cash to pay for the items you might decide to purchase them using a **credit card** (see Fig. 5.5) rather than paying by cheque. You hand your card to the retailer who records details of the card and the transaction and then issues you with a receipt. The retailer sends the bill to your bank who pay it (less their handling charge) and then send you a statement itemising your purchases at the end of each month. You check this with the receipts. Providing you pay within 21 days there is no interest payable. Why choose this method of purchasing items? You will recall that your employer benefited by paying wages directly into your current account because his money earned interest for a couple of extra days. You can do the same. By using the credit card you can delay paying for purchases for perhaps six weeks. During this period the money can be in your deposit account earning interest. If, however, you fail to pay all the outstanding bill within the 21 day period you will pay interest and this is considerably higher than the interest rates on most loans or hire-purchase transactions.

You have now set up home. Suddenly you find you have financial problems when a number of bills arrive and you discover you had not budgeted for them. The sum in your current account is insufficient to pay for them. You visit your local bank manager. He agrees to an overdraft but suggests that you ought to make plans to avoid this problem in future. He suggests a **budget account.** This will help you pay bills that are regular but vary in amount – such as gas and electricity. The bank will calculate your yearly expenditure on such bills and divide this figure by 12 (e.g. £240 ÷ 12 = £20). The resulting figure (in our example £20) is transferred every month from the current account to the budget account so that when the bills arrive there are sufficient funds to meet them. If there is not there are automatic overdraft facilities. There are numerous miscellaneous banking services open to the individual. Find out what these are when you visit the bank to check on interest rates.

Examination questions

1. In one particular month a young couple found themselves in financial difficulties due to gas, electric and telephone bills coinciding with a repair on the car, renewal of the road fund tax, annual subscription to the RAC, and TV licence. The bank manager, having assured himself that their joint income was sufficient to meet their outgoings, advised them of two services which the bank offered which would help them to avoid this problem in the future.
   Describe the **two** most appropriate banking services to help this couple.

   (Q. 2   1977)

2. What is the essential difference between hire-purchase and a bank loan?

   (Q. 1(g)   1976)

3. A relative who is purchasing a car cannot decide between hire-purchase, a bank loan or a bank overdraft as the means of financing this acquisition. Explain each option to him giving guidance as to the advantages and disadvantages of each method of finance.

   (Q. 7   1975)

4. Explain simply what the term 'collateral' means in banking.

   (Q. 1(i)   1978)

   Selecting **three** of the following pairs, explain their difference in meaning:
   (i)   commercial banks and merchant banks;
   (ii) loans and overdrafts;
   (iii) standing orders and credit transfers;
   (iv) deposit accounts and current accounts.

   (Q. 5   1978)

5. A friend is able to save a pound or two each week from her wages and tells you that she is saving for another 18 months when she is due to get married. She has already saved £190 which she keeps at home in a drawer. Give her advice on **three** alternative ways she can save in a more productive and secure manner.

(Q. 8   1978)

6. Outline the main services offered by the commercial banks and explain briefly features of their operation which distinguish them from other forms of commercial enterprise.

(Q. 11   1974)

7. Imagine you are about to purchase your first house. You pay a visit to a building society or a bank to discuss the possibility of obtaining a mortgage. What are the likely questions the manager will want answered before granting your request?

(Q. 2   1976)

8. How does a building society function? Why does a change in commercial bank interest rates affect a building society's deposit rate, and the interest rate charged on mortgages?

(Q. 4   1979)

9. What is a banker's draft?

(Q. 1(b)   1983)

10. Your employer, a bank manager, dictates the following letter:
    Dear Mr. Nethercott,
    In answer to your query I would recommend a <u>loan</u> rather than an <u>overdraft</u>, but in either case we will require <u>collateral.</u>
    Yours sincerely,

    Explain the terms underlined.

(Q. 6   1981)

International trade

Chapter 6

International trade is an unfamiliar concept to most students. To help understanding therefore, let us start off by considering a situation with which students are familiar, namely a typical household.

In our household both parents are working. The husband is an insurance broker. As you will see in Chapter 10 this involves selling insurance policies to the public in return for which the broker receives a commission from the insurance company. His wife is in business as a sole trader, selling home-made pottery. In the past they have purchased ordinary shares in a number of companies. These companies have been successful and profitable and the family's income for the current year has been boosted by the dividends received. The family has also received interest on the deposit account which they hold with a well-known bank. To assist with his job the husband wishes to buy a new car and has therefore borrowed £1,000 from his wife's parents. His own parents are retired but cannot claim supplementary benefit because they have £5,000 in the bank. They therefore give their son the £5,000 so that they can claim; he agrees to repay the £5,000 should they ever need it. The family's income could therefore be presented as in Table 6.1.

Table 6.1   Family income

	(£)
Wife's earnings	6,000
Husband's earnings	10,000
Dividends	600
Interest from bank	200
Loan from wife's parents	1,000
	£17,800
Deposit from parents	5,000

We now know where the family's income comes from. How is it

spent? Part of it goes on goods. We have already noted that the family intends to purchase a car, and other items purchased may include a washing machine or a video recorder. In addition a large proportion of the family income will be spent on food and on heating. As the family house has oil-fired central heating oil will need to be bought regularly. In addition the husband has a number of insurance policies on his life and the premiums on these need paying as does the interest payable on a mortgage on the family home. Before the end of their financial year they discover that they have a £1,500 surplus. They spend £1,000 on a holiday abroad and decide to invest £250 in shares and place £250 in the deposit account.

From the above it is possible to list the family's expenditure as shown in Table 6.2.

Table 6.2   Family expenditure

	(£)
Car, Washing Machine, Video etc	12,000
Food	3,000
Oil	500
Holiday	1,000
Interest on mortgage, premiums on insurance policy	800
Shares, money invested in deposit account	500
	£17,800

We have already seen that when a family has a surplus, that is income exceeds expenditure, then this surplus will go into its reserves, either into a bank account, a building society account or possibly invested in stocks and shares. Where however there is a deficit and its yearly expenditure exceeds the income then the difference must be made up by drawing from the reserves. Money must be withdrawn from the various accounts or the shares which it holds must be sold. If the family is in the unfortunate position of having exhausted its reserves then it must borrow funds, either from family or friends or by obtaining an overdraft from the bank. Both of these methods of financing a deficit are short-term only as loans must eventually be repaid. In the long term the family must balance its books by making its income equal its expenditure and it can do this by either increasing the income which it receives or by reducing its expenditure.

Let us now consider the financial position of a country. Where does a country's income come from? The answer is that most of the income arises from selling goods and services to other countries. Our wife earned money by selling pottery. A country earns money by selling a wide range of goods. If it is an underdeveloped country these will be raw materials, but in the developed Western world it is more likely to be manufactured goods (although in the United Kingdom the most important commodity now sold is oil). As goods can be seen they are referred to as *visibles* and when items are sold abroad they are said to be exported (the Latin 'ex' means 'out of'). Goods sold abroad are therefore called *visible* exports.

Part of the family income was derived from the husband's job as an insurance broker. He did not sell goods, he was selling a service. A country can also earn income by selling its services. Thus Lloyds of London sell insurance to the rest of the world. It is an export but, unlike goods, there is nothing tangible to be seen, it is therefore referred to as an *'invisible'* export.

The family also derived income from dividends from ordinary shares and from interest from deposit accounts. A country has the same source of income. In the past the United Kingdom (through its citizens) may have invested funds in overseas companies. If these are successful and declare dividends then the dividends are sent to the citizens in the United Kingdom. It is also possible that funds have been invested in overseas banks and again if the interest is sent back to the United Kingdom it forms part of its income.

Our family's income for the year under consideration was boosted by the £5,000 which was given to them by his parents. It will be recalled that this money was given to the family for 'financial' reasons and because they could have been asked to repay it at any time in the future they considered it prudent not to spend it. Just as people outside the family have deposited money with the family which must be repaid at a later date, so foreigners may deposit money in a country which similarly has to be repaid. They usually do this because they can obtain high rates of interest by depositing money in UK banks or because they believe that changes in a country's exchange rate could lead to them making a profit. This cash deposited in a country increases its income but because it must be returned, a country would, like the family, be unwise to spend it.

Finally, suppose that the wife formed a company in which another party bought shares. The money paid for the shares would boost the family's income for the year under consideration but it will mean that in future years part of the income from the business will need to be paid out to the investors in the form of dividends. When foreigners buy shares this again leads to an inflow of funds but, as with our family, means that income in the form of dividends will flow out in following years.

Having generated a given level of income how does a country spend it? Just as the family buys goods so a country will purchase goods from abroad (imports goods) in the form of raw materials and manufactured goods. Imported goods fall into two basic categories. The first are those which a country cannot produce for itself (many raw materials fall into this category) and secondly those which a country can produce itself, but where consumers prefer imported goods because they are cheaper, better made etc. Most developed countries possess a domestic car industry but nevertheless many imported cars will be sold because the consumer prefers them, perhaps because of their better reputation, reliability or design.

In addition to goods, a country will purchase services such as shipping, insurance or tourism; these are its invisible imports. In the family's budget this would be the expenditure on a foreign holiday.

Funds may also leave the country as dividends to overseas investors or as interest on money which has been deposited in this country. In addition British citizens may decide to invest their funds abroad either in stocks and shares or in bank accounts. While this is an expenditure in the current year it will generate income in the following year.

We have seen how a country may generate income and the ways in which it can be spent. We are now in a position to draw up a country's accounts. Where money comes into the United Kingdom this is clearly beneficial and hence is signified by a plus symbol. Where money flows out of the United Kingdom this is bad and hence is represented by a minus symbol.

In the accounts similar items are grouped together which makes for ease of comparison (see Table 6.3).

Table 6.3   UK accounts

1.	Goods exported	+ 100	
2.	Goods imported	− 90	
	Balance of trade	+ 10	This is the difference between visible imports and visible exports (i.e. goods).
3.	Services exported and dividends, interest paid into UK	+ 70	
4.	Services imported and dividends, interest paid to foreigners	− 40	
	Balance of Payments on Current Account	+ 40	This is the difference between all trade in goods and services.
5.	Investment, deposits of cash by UK citizens abroad	− 20	Money goes out of the country
6.	Investment and deposits of cash by foreigners in UK	+ 10	
	Balance of Payments	+ 30	This is the total of all transactions

The difference between goods exported and goods imported is called the balance of trade and when the invisibles are taken into account this is known as the balance of payments on current account. The final balance of payments is determined after the capital movements have taken place (items 5 and 6). The capital movements are basically the movements of cash into or out of the United Kingdom and are not directly linked with the sale or purchase of goods or services. They are primarily determined by interest rates and possible changes in the Exchange Rate.

Periodically trade figures are produced and published in the 'quality' newspapers. Two typical articles follow:

Trade sinks to £180m deficit

Britain sank into an unexpectedly deep current account deficit of £180 million in April and also experienced what is believed to be the first quarterly deficit on trade in manufactured goods for more than 100 years. News of the deficits was contained yesterday in the latest monthly trade figures.

The U.K. normally has to earn a big surplus on trade in manufactured goods in order to pay for unavoidable imports of food and raw materials . . .

In April the U.K. recorded a deficit on "visible" trade of £360 million, a very sharp deterioration from the £384 million surplus of March. . . . But after allowing for an estimated surplus of £180 million on "invisibles" like banking and tourism, the current account deficit came out at £180 million compared with a surplus of £564 million the month before.

Notes

The deficit on the balance of trade was £360m but the surplus on invisibles of £180m meant a deficit on current account of only £180m.

Only North Sea Oil keeps the picture respectable
trade figures show decline in exports.

Britain's trade performance took a severe turn for the worse last month, with further proof that only North Sea oil is keeping the trading picture moderately respectable. The latest CBI[1] monthly trends survey, out on Monday, is likely to confirm that export order books remain depressed.

The Department of Trade's figures for August reveal a visible trade deficit of £37 million against a £166 million surplus in July. The value of exports slipped back by 3½ per cent to £4,386 million, the lowest level since January. Imports were up 1 per cent or £43 million, at £4,423 million – although the surge in car imports and certain other goods such as videos continued. The picture was redeemed by another record sur-

plus on the oil account of £484 million, up from £401 million in July. And an estimated £200 million surplus on Britain's invisible trade pulled the current account up into a £163 million surplus last month, compared with £366 million in July.

The official figures confirm that the decline in Britain's export performance started in the spring. In the three months from June to August there was a visible trade surplus of £122 million, against £370 million in the previous three-month period – mainly due to a larger deficit in the non-oil account.

There were deteriorations in the balance of trade in food, beverages and tobacco and semi-manufactured goods of over £100 million in each category over the last three month period. The surplus on trade in oil improved by £100 million to reach £1 billion while there was a small improvement in the balance of trade in cars, despite the predominance of imports in the U.K. market.

Notes

1. To discover who the CBI are, turn to page 13.
2. If you rewrite the figures into the format on page 65 you obtain:

Goods exported	4,386 + [oil sales = 484]
imported	4,423 −
Balance of trade	37 −
Surplus on invisibles	200 +
Balance of Payments on current account	163 +

Let us now examine the balance of payments of three hypothetical countries shown in tables 6.4, 6.5 and 6.6.

Table 6.4   Country A

Goods exported	+ 100
Goods imported	− 80
Balance of trade	+ 20
Services exported	+ 60
Services imported	− 40
Balance of payments on current account	+ 40
Investment abroad	− 160
Investment in UK	+ 40
Deposits of cash in Country A	+ 20
Balance of Payments	− 60

The balance of payments in table 6.4 shows a deficit of 60. Despite this, Country A's accounts are healthy. There is a surplus on trade, both visible and invisible of 40. The reason why country A is temporarily short of cash is that it has invested a considerable sum of money overseas while foreigners have invested a far smaller sum in it. While this may create a temporary problem, students must remember that money which is lent must be repaid. Country A is owed more than it owes. In addition interest or dividends have to be paid on the funds lent or borrowed. This is shown in the invisible accounts the following year when Country A can expect to be in surplus.

Table 6.5   Country B

Goods exported	+ 100
Goods imported	− 140
Balance of Trade *deficit*	− 40
Services exported	+ 20
Services imported	− 80
Balance of payments *on current account deficit*	− 100
Investment abroad	− 20
Investment in Country B by foreigners	+ 80
Foreign deposits of cash in Country B	+ 90
Balance of Payments	+ 50

Looking at the accounts for Country B it would appear to possess no problems. In fact the opposite is true. Although the balance of payments is in surplus, this is entirely due to the considerable sums invested or deposited in Country B by foreigners. We saw with the family that they decided not to spend the money deposited with them because they knew it would have to be repaid in later years. If they had spent it then the money borrowed would have had to have been repaid out of their income. What is prudent for a family is also prudent for a country. Country B has had 170 invested and deposited in it by foreigners, but the country could be required to repay this sum at any time. Unlike our family however they have used this money to purchase goods and services. A re-examination of the figures will show that only 120 was earned selling goods and services while 220 was actually spent. The short fall was made up by using the money deposited by foreigners. Country B's problems will start when they are called upon to repay this sum.

Country C (Table 6.6) has a deficit on the balance of trade and yet is still in a favourable overall position because the surplus on invisibles more than compensates for this, giving a balance of payments on current account surplus. In the past this country might have achieved a surplus on the balance of payments which has led to money being invested overseas. Interest and dividends now payable on this swell the invisible surplus to compensate for the deficiency on the balance of trade. There is a surplus on the other items but as noted above, this should be discounted because it will need repayment at some later date.

Table 6.6   Country C

Goods exported	+ 100
Goods imported	− 160
Balance of trade deficit	− 60
Services exported	+ 100
Services imported	− 20
Balance of payments on current account surplus	+ 20
Investment abroad	− 20
Investment in Country C by foreigners	+ 40
Foreign deposits of Cash in Country C	+ 20
Balance of payments	+ 60

Exercise. Study the items set out below and say whether you think items listed under (a) are visible/invisible; under (b) are imports/exports.

(a) *Visible or invisibles?*

1. Cars
2. Oil
3. Tobacco
4. Money spent by tourists
5. Insurance premiums
6. Whisky

(b) *Imports (+) or Exports (−)*

7. Money spent by an American tourist in your country
8. A car sold to a foreign country
9. Oil purchased from Saudi Arabia
10. Insurance premium paid by you to a foreign company
11. Hire by you of a foreign ship
12. Purchase of Californian wine

(Answers can be found at the end of the chapter.)

It should now be appreciated that a country must achieve a surplus on its current account in the long term. Sometimes, however, a deficit or even small surplus on visible and invisibles is turned into a large deficit because of items 5 and 6 of Table 6.3 (see page 65). Where this happens the country has the same two options as a household. It can either take money from its reserves or borrow. In the family situation the latter is achieved by obtaining an overdraft or loan. The same is basically true of a country except that instead of going to a commercial bank it goes to an international bank called the International Monetary Fund

(IMF). This body provides loans to a country which is experiencing balance of payments problems to give it time to take remedial action. The following article details a Brazilian application to the IMF.

Brazil seeks IMF loan of $6.7 billion

Brazil has told the International Monetary Fund it is seeking $6.7 billion of credits over the next three years, the largest sum ever sought by a borrowing country.

This emerged during preliminary talks between a three-man IMF team and Brazilian financial officials in Brasilia.

The actions which can be taken to remedy balance of payments problems are the reduction of expenditure or increasing income.

1. To reduce expenditure

How can this be done? The public could be asked to buy fewer foreign goods and firms could be encouraged to place orders with domestic producers rather than going overseas. If this fails to reduce expenditure on imported goods then the government can limit the number of goods coming into the country by using a quota. A quota involves setting a limit on the number of items imported. If 25,000 Japanese cars are sold a month, then the government may decide to fix a quota of 5,000 cars a month. This would cut the import bill by 80 per cent.

Another option open to the government would be to impose tariffs on imported goods. A tariff is simply a tax. If a 10 per cent tariff is put on all imported cars this automatically will raise their price by 10 per cent. This makes the items more expensive compared with domestically produced goods and so the demand for imported goods will fall.

One of Britain's leading chemicals manufacturers claims that annual sales of £10m are being lost and several hundred jobs in Scotland put at risk because of unfair competition from the French. According to BP Chemicals, its continental rivals are being protected by a tax on imports and aided by subsidies on exports. The company – part of the British Petroleum empire – has demanded swift action by the European Commission to end what it calls 'these iniquitous practices'.

While tariffs may reduce demand by increasing prices, they will also increase the rate of inflation and with both quotas and tariffs there is always the possibility of retaliation by other countries.

PM attacks steel curb

Mrs Thatcher, the Prime Minister, yesterday called the US Government's imposition of a new clampdown on steel imports deplorable, and said Britain would raise the issue with US trade representative, William Brock. . . .

In Washington, Mr. Brock acknowledged that some steel firms may have valid cases in their efforts to overturn the new restrictions. . . . This was because of the complexity of the steel industry and the difficulty in deciding which companies used unfair practices to capture part of the US steel market. Because of this complexity, "your net is going to catch some who are not engaged in unfair practices." . . . But the four-year schedule of tariffs and quotas announced by a Reagan Administration on Tuesday were necessary to combat unfair foreign subsidies to the speciality steel industry.

The government may also make imported goods more expensive without using tariffs. The same effect can be achieved by devaluing the home currency.

Devaluation means that your currency is worth less in terms of other currencies. If you live in the United Kingdom you can discover the value of the £ by looking in a daily newspaper where you will find that the £'s value is given against other currencies (see table 6.7).

Table 6.7

Foreign exchanges	Tourist rates – Bank sells				
Austria	27.70	Greece	134.00	Portugal	180.00
Belgium	80.00	Ireland	1.265	Spain	222.00
Canada	1.835	Italy	2.350	Sweden	11.72
Denmark	14.32	Malta	0.64	Switzerland	3.20
France	11.90	Netherlands	4.42	USA	1.49
Germany	3.94	Norway	11.08	Yugoslavia	180.00

The table indicates how much of another currency £1 will purchase.

Thus £1 buys: 3.94 Deutschmarks
                11.90 francs
                1.49 dollars
                     pesetas
(Insert the figure and check the answer (c) on page 77).

If the £ is devalued it means that it will buy less, thus a 10 per cent devaluation would mean that it would buy 10 per cent less Deutschmarks, francs, dollars etc. Therefore:

        £1 buys 10.70 francs
        £1 buys 3.54 Deutschmarks
        £1 buys 1.34 dollars
        £1 buys   pesetas
(Insert the figures; check the answer (d) on page 77).

What effect therefore would a devaluation of the £ (we say the £ is 'getting weaker') have on the UK balance of payments?

Firstly, it would tend to increase exports because it has made our goods cheaper to foreigners. Suppose a UK word processor cost £4,000. If a Frenchman wishes to purchase it then at an exchange rate of £1 = 10 francs he must give up 40,000 francs. When the £ is devalued the Frenchman only has to give up 9 francs to obtain £1 instead of the 10 which he previously had to pay. This means that to obtain £4,000 he only has to pay 36,000 francs; the devaluation in effect means that the word processor is now 10 per cent cheaper.

It follows from the above that while the devaluation will encourage exports it will tend to discourage imports by making them more expensive. Let us consider the cost of a French Renault car. This may cost 63,000 francs. On the exchange rate of 10 francs for £1, somebody in the UK would have to give up £6,300 to obtain enough francs to purchase the Renault. When the exchange rate falls so that only 9 francs is obtained for £1 then in order to obtain 63,000 francs he will be forced to give up £7,000 (7,000 x 9). The devaluation has therefore had the effect of making the French Renault relatively more expensive. It is therefore reasonable to assume that a number of potential Renault purchasers will be dissuaded by the higher price and will turn to buying an English car instead.

A devaluation will therefore probably result in a reduction in imports while there will be an expansion in exports. This should result in improved balance of payments figures and because there is a higher demand for home-produced goods this should result in a reduction in the numbers of unemployed.

If the £ grew stronger (i.e. it bought more of a foreign currency) then

British Travel still in the red

British tourism account continued to show a deficit in the autumn, according to the latest estimates of the Department of Trade. And the rise of the pound against European currencies meant British tourists flocked back to Europe and especially to the remembered Spanish resorts of yesteryear, as it made Spanish holidays cheaper to UK holiday makers.

And although spending by tourists to Britain barely kept pace with inflation, British tourists spent considerably more abroad in October last year than 12 months previously. Overseas visitors spent £305 million in Britain, a 7 per cent increase, and UK visitors spent £365 million overseas, a 13 per cent rise on October, 1981. As a result, the UK travel account, one of the crucial components of the balance of payments, was in deficit by £60 million last October compared with a £40 million deficit in the same month of 1981.

We have examined what devaluation is, but why does it occur?

the opposite would happen. If you read the following article you will see what happened when the £ grew stronger against foreign currencies (as well as learning more about tourism as part of our invisible trade).

Government policy

If the balance of payments is in deficit the government may decide that devaluation is the answer and as will be seen in a later chapter a government may use devaluation in an attempt to reduce unemployment.

Market forces

These may also be responsible for a change in the value of a country's currency. What do we mean by market forces? Let us assume that there are a number of Englishmen who wish to buy French wine, while there are a group of Frenchmen who are interested in purchasing English cars. The French wine grower will want payment in francs and the English car manufacturer will want payment in sterling. The customers for the wine however only have sterling, while the Frenchmen wishing to buy English cars will have francs. The solution therefore is for the Frenchmen wishing to purchase the cars to exchange their currency with the Englishmen wishing to purchase wine. The Frenchman gets his sterling and the Englishman gets his francs. The question remaining therefore, is at what rate should this exchange take place?

UK citizens are buying francs worth £100   French citizens are buying sterling worth 1,000 francs

agreed rate £1 = 10 francs (1,000 ÷ 10)

In the above example UK citizens wish to exchange £100 into francs and Frenchmen wish to transfer 1,000 francs into sterling. This can be achieved at an exchange rate of £1 = 10 francs. Suppose now that there is an increased demand in the UK for French wine. Prospective purchasers of wine now wish to transfer £200 into francs. The French demand for sterling, however, has remained unaltered.

UK citizens buy francs worth £200   French citizens buy sterling worth 1,000 francs

exchange rate £1 = 5 francs.

The value of the £ has therefore fallen. Instead of purchasing 10 francs it can now only purchase 5 francs while the value of the franc has increased (this is called a revaluation). The change has occurred because the demand for francs has risen. Thus when the demand for a currency increases its value will rise. If the demand falls the opposite is true. If the demand for English cars had risen, the following might have occurred.

UK buy francs £100   French buy sterling 2,000
exchange rate £1 = 20 francs

The demand for sterling has risen hence the change in exchange rates and the revaluation of the £ (£1 will now purchase more foreign currency).

Where a currency has been revalued it will make imports cheaper whilst it will make that country's goods more expensive to foreigners. It becomes more difficult to export. The combination of these two elements means that the balance of payments will worsen. It is for this reason that when a country has a very healthy surplus on the balance of payments, its trading partners (i.e., those who have a deficit on their balance of payments) are likely to ask that country to revalue.

As explained earlier in the chapter a devaluation can cause inflation by increasing the prices of imported goods. For this reason a government may be reluctant to see its currency fall in value. They may therefore 'intervene' in the foreign exchange markets to support their currency. What happens is they use their reserves to buy their currency on the foreign exchange market. This helps it to maintain its value against other currencies. Thus

UK citizens are buying francs   French citizens are buying
worth £100   sterling worth 1,000 francs
agreed rate £1 = 10 francs

The demand for sterling remains constant but there is a greater demand in the UK for francs to pay for increased imports. Thus

UK citizens buy francs woth £200 French citizens buy sterling
            worth 1,000 francs
agreed rate £1 = 5 francs

To avoid this fall in the exchange rate the UK government can use its reserves (which it holds in francs, dollars etc). It changes 1,000 francs into sterling. Thus

UK citizens buy francs worth £200 French buy sterling worth
            2,000 francs
agreed rate £1 = 10 francs.

Such an exercise means using your reserves and this can result in them falling to a dangerously low level. In this situation a government might be forced to borrow as the following article indicates.

The French Government moved to rescue[1] the franc yesterday with a $4 billion standby loan from international banks, believed to be a record for a commercial loan to a sovereign state. The Bank of France's foreign exchange reserves had fallen from £2.7 billion to £1.9 billion since the end of July and at the present rate would have been exhausted in two months. They are now doubled at a stroke, but at a heavy cost if the standby has to be used. . . .

The cabinet also promised a new export drive to reduce the alarming trade gap, which has threatened to increase from £5 billion to £8 billion by the year end. The government policy of stimulating purchasing power through increased minimum wages, pensions and family allowance has swollen imports without helping exports.

Note

1. i.e. stop it being devalued.

It should be clear from the above that anything which affects the demand for a currency will lead to a change in its value. Some of the factors which affect demand are:

(a) A deficit

If a country has a deficit (as in the article about France) this means that it imports more than it exports. If the UK has a deficit it follows that more people will want to sell sterling to buy foreign currencies (to pay for the imports) than will wish to buy sterling. The examples above show that when this happens the £ will become worth less and will be devalued.

(b) The price of oil

If the supply of oil exceeds demand for it then in order to sell their production the oil-producing countries will be forced to lower the price in an attempt to increase demand. A lower price will mean less income for oil-producing countries, whilst at the same time it will reduce the import bill of industrialised nations such as West Germany which imports oil. This will be reflected in the balance of payments on the countries involved. If a reduction in oil prices is imminent then the value of the mark will change (it will become worth more) in anticipation of the improvement in the German balance of payments.

(c) An election

If there is a General Election in a country and the policies of one of the parties involved is believed to be detrimental to the balance of payments or they propose a devaluation, then foreigners will be reluctant to hold sterling. Companies and individuals deposit funds in banks to earn interest (see item 5 in the balance of payments table on page 65) and where there are fears of a possible devaluation the money will be removed and invested in a country which has a strong currency. The possibility of the election of a party which wants a strong currency will have the opposite effect as shown in the following article.

Pound continues upward thrust

The pound went on upwards yesterday as optimism about inflation was piled on top of the City's buoyant belief that Mrs Thatcher is certain to win the election and follow strict policies that will please the financial markets.

(d) Changes in world interest rates

As mentioned earlier in the chapter, money is deposited in countries to earn interest. If the UK rate of interest falls in relationship to the rest of the world, then companies and individuals will remove their funds from the UK to invest them in other countries where they can achieve a higher rate of interest. They will be seeking to transfer their sterling into say francs, hence the demand for francs will rise and the demand for sterling will fall. In fact everyone will be wishing to sell sterling. Apart from affecting item 5 (see page 65) in the balance of payments this will result in 'pressure' on the £ and its value against other currencies will fall.

2. To increase income

So far in order to remedy the balance of payments problem we have been primarily concerned with reducing the value of imports. The alternative remedy is to increase a country's income by increasing the amount it exports. A devaluation may help to increase sales by making the goods more competitive in price, but there are other ways to improve competitiveness. A government might decide to expand the home economy so that companies can obtain the benefits of economies of scale. As is seen in Chapter 8 companies can gain advantages from size. The research and development costs can be spread over more items and it may be in a better position to introduce new technology. The car industry is often quoted as a good example and if a government were to reduce credit restrictions this might encourage the sale of cars on the home market. If the increased sales resulted in economies of scale this would enable the firm to be more competitive in overseas markets. A government might also attempt to encourage domestic firms to export by giving grants to encourage research. It might promote trade fairs, and a close examination of newspapers will show that when government ministers visit abroad they are frequently engaged in selling British products and it is not uncommon for large orders to follow close on a ministerial visit.

Thus while the Prime Minister is understood to have clinched several notable orders on her visit to China, India is now looking to the Soviet Union for some projects and the Nigerian[1] market is likely to shrink to half its previous size this year following the imposition of import controls.

Note

1. Nigeria's solution to her balance of payments problems is to impose import tariffs and quotas.

Answers

(a)   1. Visible
      2. Visible
      3. Visible
      4. Invisible
      5. Invisible
      6. Visible
(b)   7. Export [+]
      8. Export [+]   money flows in
      9. Import [−]
     10. Import [−]
     11. Import [−]   money flows out
     12. Import [−]
(c) 222 pesatas
(d) 200 pesatas

Examination questions

1. Explain, giving examples, the term **invisible exports;** could there be **invisible imports**?

   (Q. 8   1972)

2. Why is the North Sea so important for the United Kingdom?

   (Q. 1(c)   1974)

3. What is the difference between 'visible' and 'invisible' trade?

   (Q. 1(j)   1974)

4. Examine the main advantages to be derived from international trade.

   (Q. 5   1974)

5. Is money spent by an American tourist in London, UK, a British import or a British export? Briefly explain your reasoning.

(Q. 1(a)   1976)

6. What is the difference between a quota and a tariff?

(Q. 1(c)   1976)

7. 'The pound has fallen against the American dollar.' Does this make our exports cheaper for Americans to buy, or more expensive? Briefly explain.

(Q. 1(a)   1977)

8. 'Although the balance of trade is in deficit the overall balance of payments is favourable.' Briefly explain how this could be so.

(Q. 1(b)   1977)

9. Give a simple explanation of why 'gold and foreign currency' reserves are so important to the value of a nation's currency.

(Q. 1(h)   1978)

10. What precisely is meant by the 'Trade Gap'?

(Q. 1(i)   1978)

11. Discuss **four** ways in which an adverse balance of payments may be corrected.

(Q. 2   1978)

12. State two ways in which a country might finance a balance of payments deficit.

(Q. 1(a)   1983)

13. Study the following figures extracted from the Balance of Payments for the United Kingdom

	Units
Goods exported	100
Goods imported	120
Services exported	40
Services imported	110
Overseas investment in UK	140
Overseas deposits of cash in UK	160

(a) Calculate (i) the Balance of Trade
           (ii) the Balance of Payments on current account.

(b) If sterling were devalued by 10% what effect might this have on the figures?

(c) If UK interest rates fell how might this affect the figures?

(Q. 5   1983)

Business organisation: I
Chapter 7

A young college lecturer is anxious to improve his family's standard of living and so decides to set up a business. He intends to produce cassette tapes on various topics which can then be purchased by students so that they can study in their own homes. He will then be the sole owner of the business and therefore can retain all the profits that he makes. He is in fact **a sole trader.**

This is the simplest type of business to start, requiring no legal formalities. Its main feature is that it is owned by one person, hence the name, although the owner may employ his own staff and a sole trader can become relatively large. They are primarily found in the retail trade, the service trades (such as hairdressers, plumbers, window cleaners and beauticians) and the professions (such as solicitors and architects).

Our young college lecturer faces two main problems in setting up his business. The first is that he possesses unlimited liability. This means that his liability is not limited to the amount that he has invested in the business. If the business makes a loss then its creditors can claim his personal assets if the business assets are insufficient to pay the debts. Thus he may lose his house, car, furniture and other personal effects.

His other problem is also financial. Where can he obtain the finance to start the business and how can he afford to live until the business becomes profitable? Setting up a business costs money. In the above example, a recording studio will have to be hired, readers will have to be paid, scripts will have to be written and authors paid.

Cassette tapes will have to be purchased and facilities for their production organised. The sole trader may provide the finance himself or he may turn to other sources, perhaps relatives or friends. He may even try to obtain a bank loan, but as you will remember from Chapter 5 the bank is unlikely to give a loan unless the debtor can provide collateral or a guarantor. The problems of raising capital means that sole traders usually start with a limited capital and in the early days many sole traders start from their own homes. This avoids the need to purchase or rent premises and it will help if the business chosen requires little equipment. The window cleaner needs only a bucket and a ladder whereas the hairdresser will require a range of expensive equipment.

Businesses do not become immediately profitable. There is often a significant time lapse before a business produces income. The cassette tapes must be purchased, the recording studio paid and the readers' fees paid long before the tapes can be sold to the public. In this period between the capital expenditure and the receipt of income, the sole trader must live. In our example, he has his full-time job to support him but many sole traders have become bankrupt because they have failed to take into account the need to pay the bills before they receive any income.

Let us assume however, that our sole trader has managed to overcome the financial problems and is now successfully trading. Rather than trade under his own name he has decided to call his business Barl Enterprises. The business has expanded and is so successful that the sole trader suddenly finds himself paying more than the standard rate of taxation. He also requires additional help to run the business and is seeking to increase the capital invested in the business so that he can expand the range of tapes offered. He therefore decides to form a **partnership.**

A partnership consists of two or more people who join together in a business enterprise. The lecturer takes on his wife as an **active partner.** This means that she plays an active role in the business. She will take the responsibility for despatching tapes to meet the orders and keep the financial accounts. She is to receive one quarter of the profits of the enterprise (the division of the profits is usually found in the Deed of Partnership), as this reduces the tax liability of her husband. Everybody is entitled to earn a certain sum of money without paying tax (in 1984 a wife was allowed to earn £2,005) and so by transferring at least this amount to his wife, he can avoid paying tax.

For the same reason he intends to make his mother a partner. She does not intend to get involved in the running of the business and therefore she is known as a **sleeping partner.** She still, however, shares in the profits and losses.

The lecturer also intends to offer a partnership to a family friend who has agreed to contribute the extra capital. This friend is, however concerned that all partners, like sole traders, possess unlimited liability. As he does not wish to become involved in the running of the business he is worried that if the active partners make the wrong decisions (and the partnership becomes bankrupt) he could lose his personal possessions. It is therefore agreed that he should become a **limited partner.** This means that although he contributes capital and shares in the profits and losses, he can take no active part in the running of the business and therefore receives limited liability. In our example this is possible because at least one of the partners possesses unlimited liability.

Hairdressing is an area where sole traders are common. The owner of 'Panache', your local hairdressing salon, wishes to expand and purchase the adjoining shop as a beauty salon. The owner has no experience of beauty work and is unable to finance the purchase through her own resources. She therefore decides to take on a partner who is an experienced beautician and who is prepared to bring into the partnership sufficient funds for the purchase of the adjoining premises. This produces two of the advantages of a partnership: an expansion of capital and greater management expertise. Both partners will, however, possess unlimited liability and as either partner can enter into contracts which bind the other, it is important that they trust each other. Because trust is important in a partnership, if one partner dies or becomes bankrupt the partnership is automatically dissolved.

Let us return to our original example of Barl Enterprises which is now a partnership selling cassette tapes. The business has continued to prosper and the partners are now considering publishing academic text books to supplement the tapes. To determine whether this expansion would be profitable, the firm must obtain the answer to four questions.

1. Is there a market? (Will people buy the books?)
To answer this the views of potential readers must be canvassed and a survey made of material already existing. The latter could be done by examining publishers' book lists and the former by issuing a survey or questionnaire to selected college lecturers and students. This question-naire may be compiled by the firm but in many organisations it is common to use a market-research firm to perform this task.

2. Can it create a suitable product at the right price?
In our example it will be books, but it could just as easily be cars, washing machines or greenhouses. With publishing a suitable author will need to be found, the length of the book determined and the type of print and layout agreed. In addition a decision must be made as to where the book will be produced, i.e. printed. These are all factors which will affect the cost. If it is possible to produce a product which fulfils the unmet needs of the consumer the firm must then consider how the product (book) is to be sold.

3. How is the product to be sold?
Will the firm use its existing mail-order business to sell the books? Will it produce a catalogue or will it go through the more traditional outlets of booksellers and multiples such as W. H. Smith? Having made the decision, the firm must then decide how it is to distribute the books to the point of sale if the latter two are used. Does it use an outside carrier or does it deliver itself?

4. How can people be persuaded to buy the product?
It will need attractive packaging (in our example a suitably attractive

cover) and will then need promoting by means of advertising and sales promotions. The choice of advertising media will depend on the size of the company and the nature of the market. With a firm selling educational textbooks, advertisements in student magazines such as Memo or in the professional teaching journals would produce a better response than advertising in one of the Sunday colour supplements.

The above four functions are the **marketing** functions within a company. In large organisations these will be provided within the business but smaller firms may well employ outside specialists to advise them on these points.

The importance of marketing is illustrated by the case of Clive Sinclair and the domestic computer. In the late 1970s he asked himself the question, 'Is there a market for a small home computer costing less than £100?' He decided the answer was 'Yes' and found that there was not a single computer on the market. He therefore designed a suitable product, the ZX81. He found a firm to manufacture it for him and decided to sell it by mail order. Outside specialists were also employed to do this. As potential purchasers were the educated middle classes, the bulk of the advertising was done in the supplements of the 'class' Sunday newspapers. By 1983, the company had sold 900,000 such computers and the originator of the company, Clive Sinclair, was estimated to be worth £127,000,000.

Sinclair surviving computer price war

Sir Clive Sinclair yesterday showed no signs of succumbing to the bitter price war in a business he created – the cheap home computer.

His company, Sinclair Research, of Cambridge, announced pre-tax profits of £14.03 million, just above the level he had forecast, and he said that this year too is "looking pretty good," Turnover doubled to £54.53 million (which represents about £1 million per direct employee) and the profit was up by 61 per cent. A dividend of 1p a share was announced, because of the need to reinvest profits.

The personal computer business ranges from the cheapest home models (Sinclair's ZX 81, for instance, now down to £40) to £10,000 and more for desktop "work stations". The most solid market is in the middle, and Sir Clive sees a new niche there. He said yesterday that he was developing a "professional computer," to be launched early next year. This will be well up market from the home computers but cheaper than the top business micros.

Sinclair Research, formed four years ago, is still 85 per cent owned by Sir Clive himself. Last February institutional investors subscribed £13.6 million for a 10 per cent holding. Sir Clive was the first (in 1980) to see the market for a cheap introductory computer costing less than £100. Today he has hundreds of imitators and competitors.

A considerable sum of money (capital) will be required to set up the publishing part of the business. The partners' personal assets are likely to prove insufficient. Where can they raise the necessary capital? They may approach the bank for a loan. Whilst this may generate sufficient funds to start the publishing venture, it will have to be repaid at some point in the future. What the partnership really requires is a permanent loan (i.e. one that does not have to be paid back). It can obtain this by becoming a company.

Company

Most companies today are created by registering under the Companies Acts. They differ from partnerships in two main ways.

Firstly, they are said to have **perpetual succession.** In a partnership if one partner dies you will remember the firm is automatically dissolved, it comes to an end. Because the number of partners is small (there is a legal limit to the number of partners a firm can have) it is fairly easy for the remaining partners to re-form the business under the same name and operate from the same trade premises. As far as customers of the partnership are concerned it will be business as usual and most of them will probably be unaware that there has been a change in ownership.

Whilst the owners of the partnership (the partners) usually number less than twenty, the number of people who have a share in a company (the shareholders) may run into hundreds of thousands. If each time one of the company's owners (shareholders) died the company was dissolved, it would create commercial chaos because all the remaining shareholders would need to be contacted before the company could be re-formed. For that reason the company has perpetual succession which means that the company continues to exist even though owners of the company (the shareholders) may die and be replaced by new shareholders.

The second difference is that shareholders possess **limited liability.** This means that if the company in which they hold shares goes bankrupt (its liabilities exceed its assets) then the shareholders' losses are limited to the amount which they have invested in the company (their shareholding). The unpaid creditors cannot claim the personal possessions of the shareholders. This protection is necessary to persuade the public to invest in companies. With a partnership each partner usually has a say in the running of the partnership. As each partner is responsible for the decisions made it is only right that they should be responsible for the profits made or losses incurred. In a company the number of shareholders is so great that, unlike partners, they cannot be involved in the day-to-day running of the company. They elect a Board of Directors to run the company on their behalf. The former are accountable to the shareholders at an Annual General Meeting. If the latter are satisfied they can re-elect the board but if they are unhappy with the decisions made in the previous year they can dismiss the Board and elect another in its place.

Rowton coup

Two directors of Rowton Hotels were thrown off the board yesterday in a surprise move led by the group's largest shareholder, Gresham House Estate. Mr. William Harris, Rowton's chairman, and a fellow director, Mr. Clive Eckert, were not re-elected at the annual meeting after a poll demanded by a representative of Gresham House which holds a 24 per cent stake. Earlier shareholders approved the sale of four Rowton hotels which will raise over £3 million. A spokesman at Hill Samuel, Rowton's advisers, said Gresham House was no longer confident in the board's ability to handle its investments. Shares in Rowton jumped 5p to 174p on speculation of a reshuffle yet to be announced.

Because the shareholders have no say in the day-to-day running of the business, it would not be possible to persuade people to invest in companies if they had unlimited liability. This would mean that in the event of a bad decision being made by the Board a person who held perhaps only a hundred pounds worth of shares could lose their house, car and other personal possessions. To overcome this problem shareholders therefore possess limited liability.

The features of perpetual succession and limited liability are found in both public and private companies. The main distinction between a public and a private company is that only the former may sell its shares to the public and have a quote on the stock exchange. For that reason it can raise larger sums in capital than the private company. It is however very expensive for a company to have a Stock Exchange quotation and therefore the medium-sized commercial or industrial company tends to be a private company. In our example, given the size of the capital required by Barl Enterprises, it would form a private company and it would not consider going 'public' until its turnover was quoted in millions, rather than thousands.

To form either type of company two documents must be filed with the Registrar of Companies. The first of these is the *Memorandum of Association*, which indicates the relationship of the company with the outside world. It therefore defines the company's powers, includes the name of the company (in the UK this is followed by the letters plc) with an indication that its members have limited liability. It also states the amount of capital which the company may raise. The other document is the *Articles of Association* which deals with the internal running of the company. It therefore covers such matters as the issue and transfer of shares, conduct of general meetings and the powers and duties of directors. These two documents are submitted to the Registrar who then issues a Certificate of Incorporation which brings the company into being.

As explained above, apart from the desire to obtain limited liability, the main reason for forming a company is the need to raise larger sums of capital than are available in a partnership. The amount of capital which a company may raise is found in the Memorandum of Association. This figure is the company's authorised capital. It is this sum which it is authorised to raise by issuing shares. In the case of Barl Enterprises this figure might be £250,000 and the Memorandum might indicate that this is to consist of £250,000 one pound shares. Having conducted their marketing exercise Barl Enterprises discover that it will only cost £125,000 to commence publishing. It would therefore issue only £125,000 from the authorised capital. This would mean that if it ever required additional funds it could issue shares up to a value of £125,000 (i.e. up to the total of the authorised capital.) Earlier in the chapter it was stated that by selling shares the company obtained a permanent loan. Once a company has issued ordinary shares it never has to buy them back although it must distribute part of its profits to its shareholders. This creates two problems for the ordinary shareholder in a public company. Firstly, how does she know how much her shareholding is worth? Secondly (as it is not possible to ask the company to redeem them) how can she transfer her shares back into cash?

How does she know what they are worth?

As the name indicates, each shareholder owns a share of the company. If there are one hundred shares and the company is valued at £1,000 then each share is worth £10. If the company's value rises to £3,000 then each share will be worth £3,000 divided by 100, which equals £30. In business of course, we are not talking about hundreds or thousands, but about hundreds of thousands and millions. If you are a shareholder

Table 7.1   Extract from the *Guardian*

Low (Wm)	274		Mgmt Ag	119	− 1
Lowe RH	a29		Mchstr Ship	141	
Lucas Inds	159	− 1	Manders	141	+ 1
MCD Group	47		Mang Brz	35	
MFI Furn	a135	− 1	Manor Mtrs	13	
MK Elec	311	− 2	Marchwiel	198	− 4
MY Dart	23		Marks & Spn	202	+ 1
Macarthys	a138	− 3	Marley	a65	
McC'dale	273		Marling Ind	a43	
Mackay (H)	63	+ 1	Marshall H	a153	+ 2
McKecknie	129	− 1	Marshalls Un	46	+ 2
Macph'son	49	− 1	Mn-Black	219	
Magnet S	a154	− 2	Martin A	46	

a = ex divided

in a public company you can discover how much your shares are worth
by looking in the 'Financial' press.

Table 7.1 is an extract from the financial pages of the *Guardian*.

Shares are listed in alphabetical order and you can see the shares in
Marks & Spencer are worth 202 which is 1p more than the previous
day.

From the above she can therefore ascertain the value of her shares
and whether they increased or decreased in the previous day's trading.
The *Financial Times* also gives other information which helps the
'professional' to decide whether to buy or sell shares. Table 7.2 is an
extract from *Financial Times* showing shares in the retailing area;
shares are grouped according to areas.

Table 7.2   Extract from *Financial Times*

Div Paid			Price	Last Div.	Div. Net	C/yr	P/E
June	Nov	Home Charm 10p	323	21.3	4.0	2.9	22.5
Dec	July	House of Fraser	200	4.0	7.5	1.9	12.0
Dec	June	House of Lerose	147	21.3	7.6	–	–
Apr	Aug	Jones (Ernest) 10p	78	7.3	3.9	0.3	–
Sept	–	+ Kean & Scott	53	6.68	1.0	–	–
Jan	July	LDH Group	14	2.6	–	–	–
Oct	Apr	Ladies Pride 20p	49	21.2	3.4	0.5	(41.6)
Aug	Nov	Lee Cooper	113 xd	1.11	3.02	6.7	4.2
May	Nov	Liberty	140	4.10	3.0	–	–
May	Nov	Do. Non Vtg Ord	90	4.10	3.0	–	–
Sept	Apr	Lincroft K. 10p	60½	21.2	2.0	2.4	12.6
Nov	Apr	MFI Furniture 10p	155	21.2	2.8	2.4	22.0
Jan	July	Marks & Spencer	204 xd	15.11	5.1	2.0	19.7
Feb	July	Martin News	195	31.12	5.78	3.1	8.7
Oct	–	Mellins 5p	142	Je 65	n–	–	–
Jan	July	Menzies (J)	323	15.11	5.0	–	–

Most of the information is only for the 'professional' investors and
students need not bother with it. They should note that the letters xd
appear against the name of Marks & Spencer and these stand for 'ex
dividend'. This means that a dividend has recently been declared
which is payable to the holders of ordinary shares. The letters signify
that if the share is sold, the dividend will be paid to the seller of the
shares and not to the new shareholder.

The general movement of all shares is indicated by the Financial
Times Index. If this is at 900 and rises to 910, this signifies a general
increase in share prices. It is, however, possible for certain shares to
move in an opposite direction from the Financial Times Index, thus the
Index may be falling although a particular share or group of shares may
have increased in price.

Why should a particular share increase in price?

We noted above that if the company's value increases then its share price will rise. Anything therefore that will improve a company's profitability and therefore its value, will tend to lead to a rise in its share price. If a company has a large export market and there is a devaluation to the pound this will probably result in an increase in its share price. A devaluation of the pound will make it cheaper for foreigners to buy UK goods and therefore the company should see an increase in sales. A company manufacturing washing machines for the home market may be threatened by cheap foreign imports. If the government introduces an Import Tariff (tax) or a Quota (limit on the number to be imported) this should result in increased sales for the domestic company, hence higher profits and therefore an increased share price.

The F.T. Index usually rises if events occur which the 'City' thinks will be favourable to the Stock Market. Consider the following newspaper article.

Buoyant city predicts Tory win

The latest opinion polls have convinced a previously cautious City that a Tory victory is now almost a certainty, and the markets yesterday pushed the pound up sharply and left shares at a new closing record.

For the first time, shares closed above 700 on the Financial Times Index, which is regarded as a landmark in the City. The index has been above this level for brief periods during trading days but never at the close of business. It ended 0.8 up at 700.6. The pound soared because of the reassurance from the polls, closing 1.65 cents up against the dollar at $1.5855, back to the level at the beginning of the year.

Of course the opposite is also true!

Share prices in Hong Kong are poised on the brink of collapse again as fears grow within the business community that the colony's relative autonomy may not, after all, be assured following the termination of the New Territories lease in 1997.

The Hong Kong market after last summer's panic, has slowly returned to normal on the belief that last September's negotiations in Peking between Mrs. Thatcher and the Chinese Government had paved the way for a settlement which would allow the colony to retain its present structure with a degree of British administration after the expiration of the lease.

This week, however, it has now been reliably disclosed that China has already drafted laws which will transform Hong Kong into a Special Administration Region without any alllowance for continued British participation.

How can shares be realised?

'Realising shares' means turning them into cash. The answer is to find another member of the public willing to buy them. In order to link the sellers with potential purchasers of shares, a market has developed. This is known as the Stock Exchange. Shareholders wishing to dispose of their shares instruct a broker to sell them on their behalf. Those wishing to buy shares will instruct a broker accordingly. Each broker will then approach a jobber on the floor of the Stock Exchange. The broker wishing to sell shares will ask the jobber to quote him a price. The jobber will quote two prices, the lower being the price he will buy shares for, and the higher one, the price at which he sells them. If the selling broker is happy with the lower price, a deal will be done and the jobber will purchase the shares for himself. At a later stage, the purchasing broker will contact the jobber and will be quoted the same prices, if he is happy he will then purchase shares at the higher price. The difference between the two prices is known as the Jobbers Turn, and is the profit he makes from the transactions. In this way, there is a ready market for ordinary shares. The division of work between brokers and jobbers has led to criticism, as is evident from the following article.

Stock exchange fights off inquiry

The Government has bowed to pressure from the City and plans to intervene to stop the Office of Fair Trading's case against the restrictive practices of the Stock Exchange. In return for this the exchange has agreed to make concessions. . . .

The concessions the exchange are prepared to make are mainly in its commission system. At present it fixes the minimum commission that members charge on deals. This means that brokers are unable to compete for business on price, but instead compete by offering extensive research to attract the large investing institutions. This guarantees large profits from the brokers most successful at getting institutional business. The exchange is believed to be prepared to phase out its minimum commission regulations over a number of years. In return for this, and for some easing of conditions of entry to the Exchange, the Exchange will be allowed to keep its unique system of having separate jobbers and brokers. The jobbers deal in the shares themselves but do not deal in London directly with investors. The brokers, who do deal with the public cannot trade in shares between each other, but are forced to go through the jobbers.

Business organisation: II
Chapter 8

Size and change

Any company, if it is to survive and remain profitable, must meet the challenge of new technology. This may mean changing the method of production by using, for example, more robots as has occurred in the motor industry, or perhaps by changing the range of products which the company offers.

> Barl Enterprises are a relatively small public company. It is 1980 and their range of products consists of manual and electric typewriters. In the early 1980s there is a movement away from traditional typewriters to electronic typewriters and word processors.
>   What is this company's response?

1. Inaction

As a result of either inertia (the company does not want to change) or ignorance (the company is unaware of the changing nature of the market), it continues to manufacture solely manual and electric typewriters. As a result it loses its market to those companies who can offer a range of electronic typewriters and word processors. Barl Enterprises will become smaller. What are the consequences?

Falling demand for its products means the company will have to cut back on the number of typewriters it produces. It will therefore need to employ less staff. The consequence of this will be redundancy. The workers who are no longer required will be made redundant and if they have worked for long enough with the company, will be given a lump sum as a redundancy payment and leave to join the ranks of the unemployed. Before the company can make a large part of its work-force redundant, however, it must inform the Trade Union. The union may decide to recommend industrial action in an attempt to preserve jobs. Such action is unlikely to involve a strike because the object of a strike would be to stop the production of typewriters and, given the falling demand, this is unlikely to embarrass the firm. A more effective weapon might be a sit-in.

Sit-in stops factory

The Sheffield engineering firm of Firth Denhon was at a standstill yesterday after 80 workers began *a sit-in over compulsory redundancies*. They warned that they would continue to occupy the factory until five compulsory redundancy notices were lifted. Workers at the factory, which make aerospace parts, have been on short time for 2½ years, and 60 jobs have been shed through voluntary redundancies over the last 15 months.

The company's problems affect not only its work-force, they also affect the owners (the ordinary shareholders). The dividend they receive and the value of their shares depends upon the profitability of the firm. As profits fall so the dividend they receive will decrease and, as you will recall from the previous chapter, as the value of the company diminishes so the value of their shares will fall. For example:

100,000 shares.   Company valued £1,000,000

Value of share $\dfrac{1,000,000}{100,000}$ = £10

100,000 shares.   Company valued £500,000

Value of share $\dfrac{500,000}{100,000}$ = £5

100,000 shares.   Company valued £100,000

Value of share   _____

Eventually the company will be forced to go into liquidation (it will be broke). In this situation its assets will be sold and its creditors paid off. Any surplus is then divided among the Debenture Holders. Any remaining sum will then be divided among the ordinary shareholders who therefore may receive nothing. If the company's assets are insufficient to pay the creditors then, because the ordinary shareholders possess limited liability, their personal assets cannot be seized by the unpaid creditors.

2. Action

Barl Enterprises is aware of the need to change. Its Marketing Department has been monitoring the sales returns from the sales representatives and conducting market research. As a result the Board of Directors are aware of the declining demand for electric and manual typewriters and the growing expansion of the electronic market. They are anxious to grasp the opportunities that are offered. The first step is therefore to assess the new consumer needs more accurately. This is another function of the Market Research Department. They will need to collect information on the type of typewriter required and, once a sample machine is produced, test it in a sample area. If the results are satisfactory the company will then arrange for a national launch. The product will be displayed at Trade Fairs and Business Exhibitions, advertised in the Trade Press and potential customers circularised.

The company will need to finance the research which is necessary before a new product can be manufactured and also the cost of setting up a new production line. Where can Barl Enterprises find the additional cash? A bank loan or overdraft could be used for temporary finance and it could re-invest profits (see earlier Sinclair press cutting), but long-term capital would probably be raised by issuing more shares. Students will recall that the Memorandum of Association includes details of the company's authorised capital. Barl Enterprises' authorised capital is £2 million, to be issued in £1 shares. In order to start trading the company only issued £1 million shares (its issued capital) and it therefore has a further one million shares which it is authorised to issue (the difference between the issued capital and the authorised capital). It can therefore raise additional funds by the issue of further shares. If, however, the company had already issued £2 million of shares, then a further issue of shares could only be made with the permission of the Registrar of Companies. Barl Enterprises decides to issue the whole £1 million in £1 shares. How can it do this? The most common way is through an offer 'for sale'. This means offering the new shares to the general public at a fixed price.

Although the company is issuing shares with a nominal value of £1 they may be issued to the general public at £1.50. When the company was originally formed it was valued at £2 million. As it could issue two million shares, each shareholder owned one/two millionth of the company, hence the value of the share was £1. The company has been successful and as a consequence its value has risen. It is now worth £3 million. There are still only two million possible shareholders, each shareholder therefore still owns one/two millionth share in the company. This share is now however worth £1.50 (3 million divided by 2 million). The original shareholders who purchased shares for £1 can now sell them for £1.50 through their brokers on the Stock Exchange. Anybody now wishing to buy a share in the company would be expected to pay £1.50, hence the new issue would be made at this price. If the offer price is too high then the public will not purchase the shares and if it is too low the company will effectively lose money.

In our example, let us assume the offer price is £1.30. The public will appreciate the shares are undervalued and therefore the offer will be over-subscribed. The public will offer to buy six million shares although the company is only selling one million. When there is an over-subscription, the shares can be allocated in a variety of methods. In our example, the company might decide to issue one share for each six applied for. Once the shares have been issued they will be quoted on the Stock Exchange. Because the demand for shares exceeded their supply, it is likely that the price quoted on the Stock Market would be £1.50, thus enabling each lucky applicant to sell each share she purchased at a profit of twenty pence (the shares would be quoted at a premium of 20 pence above the issue price). Shares can be undervalued as indicated in the following newspaper clipping.

Superdrug's market debut has broken Eurotherm's record for oversubscription. Its offer for sale attracted a staggering £1,470 million so each share could have been sold 95 times. Eurotherm was 85 times oversubscribed. When dealings start next Wednesday, the shares are expected to go to a premium of 40p above the issue price of 175p a share.

Brothers Ronald and Peter Goldstein saw the shares of their Superdrug group soar to 295p on the first day of trading before falling back to 271p making their personal shareholdings worth £15.3 million a piece, and pricing their supermarket drugstores chain at £95 million. The shares were offered for sale last week at just 175p each and sure of a bargain stags offered an amazing £1.47 billion for the 8.8 million shares actually offered for sale – only 25 per cent of the total group. At least a dozen financial institutions were said to have subscribed for the entire issue, and with many applications being held up in the post the issue was 95 times oversubscribed. The share allocation was greatly scaled down.

A **Stag** (or a **Bull**) is a person who buys shares he believes are about to rise in price. When shares are purchased the buyer does not have to pay for them immediately. He must pay on 'settlement day'. This means that if a stag sells the newly purchased shares before settlement day he can make a profit without having to part with any money.

Consider Superdrug   Purchase 1,000 shares at 175p on 1 October
                       Settlement day 8 October
                       Sell 1,000 shares at 295p on 2 October
                       Settlement day 8 October

The Stag receives a cheque for £2,950 on 8 October from his buyer and must then write out a cheque for £1,750. He has therefore made a profit of £1,200!

A **Bear** is the opposite of a stag. He sells shares (say 1,000) which he does not own because he believes they will fall in price before settlement day. He will then buy 1,000 shares at the lower price. Thus

Sells 1,000 shares at 295p on 3 October
Settlement day 8 October
Buys 1,000 shares at 215p on 4 October
Settlement day 8 October

The **Bear** must write out a cheque for £2,150 on the 8th but the buyer must write him out a cheque for £2,950 on the same day. This gives him a profit of £800.

If, however, the Bear is wrong and the share price rises (or if the Stag finds share prices fall) he will make a loss.

Because it is important to get the issue price correct, companies offering shares to the public usually seek the professional advice of a Merchant Bank. It will advise the company on the timing of the new issue (i.e. at a time when the public want to buy shares) and the price. The company will advertise the offer in the serious Press and a prospectus will be published with an application form. The prospectus includes information on the company's history, details of the issue and profit statements for previous years. Once he has read this the potential investor will decide whether she wishes to buy the company's shares at the offer price. Apart from advising on the time and price of the offer for sale, the Merchant Bank will act as an underwriter. In the event of an offer being under-subscribed (not all the shares are sold to the public) the underwriters guarantee to purchase the unallotted shares which they will then seek to sell at some later date.

The company may, however, decide to issue the new shares to the existing shareholders by means of a Rights Issue. This means that each existing shareholder is offered one share at a favourable price (i.e. below the current market price of the shares) for each share or number of shares she holds.

Having obtained the necessary finance, the firm's management can now plan the production of the electronic typewriters. The production line for the component parts must be set up and the production process planned to avoid delays that could arise because of shortage of materials or equipment. The Personnel Department will also need to recruit additional staff and, depending on the nature of their work, train them.

The business is now producing electronic typewriters and provided it has got the product and the price right it should be able to expand. As it does so, it should become more profitable because the cost of producing each item should fall, as Table 8.1 shows.

Table 8.1

Items produced	Total cost of production	Average cost of production (i.e. total cost ÷ items produced)
1,000	100,000	100
2,000	180,000	90
3,000	255,000	85
4,000	320,000	

The reason for the fall in the average cost price of producing each item is that as the firm expands in size it can take advantage of what is referred to as the 'economies of scale'.

The first of these are the technical economies. In order to produce the electronic typewriters the business has set up a production line to make the component parts which it later assembles into the finished machines. Let us assume that the cost of setting up the production line was £100,000. This is known as a fixed cost because it does not vary with the levels of production. It remains constant. If 10,000 machines are made then each must contribute £10 towards the fixed cost (100,000 divided by 10,000). If production increases to 50,000 machines then this figure falls to £2. As production rises therefore the fixed costs (which also includes rent and rates) can be spread over a larger number of items. The increased production also enables the business to make more efficient use of its production line. If only 10,000 are being produced then one machine or one operator may be called to perform several tasks. If production rises to 50,000 machines then more specialist equipment can be used (such as robots) and the work force will also be able to specialise. This specialisation (or division of labour) enables both the employees and the machinery to be used more efficiently and therefore more cheaply. This also leads to a lowering in the average cost of production.

The second economy is marketing. You will recall that one of the functions of the marketing department is to plan the advertising campaign. This must be aimed at the potential customer. The advertising budget is therefore allocated as follows:

Advertising in trade magazines	£50,000
Stands at business exhibitions	£10,000
Sales literature	£10,000
Total cost	£70,000

If ten thousand machines are produced, then each one must contribute £7 towards the cost of advertising (70,000 divided by 10,000). If, however, the number sold increases to 35,000, then this figure falls to £2. Economies also arise in the use of the sales force. A sales representative has to be paid to cover an area and his salary could remain constant whether he sells one hundred or one thousand typewriters. You should now realise the implications this has on the price of the typewriter.

The pace of change in electronic office equipment means that the business must be engaged in research and development. They must be in a position to take full advantage of changes in technology. This will cost money. There are the salaries of the electronics engineers and the cost of designing and building the new equipment. These research costs have to be recouped from the sale of the products. If the costs are £100,000 and a thousand products are sold, each product must contribute £100. This figure will fall to £1 if 100,000 are sold. This is therefore another economy of scale.

Another advantage for the large company is that it can employ specialists. A sole trader must perform all the management functions, such as marketing and accountancy. The large organisation can employ the specialist accountant, the research engineer and the advertising specialists. Just as a company benefits from using specialist equipment so it will benefit from using specialist management.

The firm producing electronic typewriters may expand by taking an increasing share of the market. Growth may also be achieved if it amalgamates with a firm producing a similar product. This would occur if Imperial amalgamated with Canon. This would be an example of **horizontal integration.** The larger firm may be able to achieve greater economies of scale and if it has a sufficiently large share of the market it may be in a monopoly position. By being the only or one of the very few suppliers it may be able to increase profits by charging higher prices.

Our firm does not sell its electronic typewriters directly to businesses, but uses specialist office equipment retailers. With increasing competition from other firms it is worried that these retailers might promote competitors' models instead of its machines. To avoid this situation the firm decides to **take over** (buy) Town and Country Office Supplies Limited who have a nationwide selling organisation. This is an example of **vertical integration,** which entails a company taking over firms who are involved with the prior stages in the business or, as is the case here, in the later stages. Another example would be petrol stations taking over garages or breweries controlling public houses.

Being large, can however, have its disadvantages. It can often result in problems with the staff. Employees who feel part of a firm are likely to work harder and take fewer days off. As organisations grow there is a tendency for them to become more impersonal and for a rift to develop between management and employees. This can result in anti-management feeling and the possible growth of a militant trade union. Management will of course attempt to overcome these potential problems by better communications with the work-force. As indicated in Chapter 2, communications are a vital tool in improving staff morale and motivation, but as organisations grow in size so the barriers to effective communications grow.

As Managing Director of the electronics firm I am concerned about the quality of the typewriters being manufactured. Many customers are now complaining of poor quality and faulty workmanship. This matter must be brought to the attention of the work-force. I know what has to be said and I appreciate that it has to be put over to the work-force in such a way that it will produce a positive response in them. In a small one-man business I can go and talk to the workers and probably solve the problem. In a large organisation the Managing Director will have a director in charge of production; he will have managers working for him and below them there will be supervisors and finally the work-force. In communicating we have already discussed the need to be aware of staff feelings. Suppose I as Managing Director call a meeting of the production workers and discuss with them the quality of the work being produced. What effect will this have on their supervisors, the managers, and the Production Director? I have by-passed them to talk directly with the work-force and this may be interpreted as a lack of confidence in the ability of the managers, supervisors etc. Within any organisation there is a chain of communication and a failure to use this may affect the morale of those by-passed. If I do use it however then the message which I wish to have relayed to the work-force will have to pass through a number of people. This increases the chance of the message being distorted or not passed on. It is in a situation like this that 'send reinforcements' becomes 'send three and fourpence'.

It is not only internal communications that may be adversely affected. Size may also make communication between the firm and its customers more difficult. Bureaucracy and red tape are often a feature of size. The potential customer who phones up to place an order may often be passed from department to department as nobody wishes to take the responsibility for making a decision, or fobbed off with the excuse, he will phone you back (pyb!) Unable to get a satisfactory answer the potential customer may become frustrated and turn to the small firm where he can soon be put into personal contact with the appropriate person and possibly a decision can be made over the telephone.

Large-scale production, while technically efficient, demands specialisation by employees which we noted earlier was called division of labour. Each employee does one task and it is claimed that constant repetition makes him quicker and more efficient. It is also likely that the job will become boring and tedious. The employee will become frustrated. Below are the views of a car worker, taken from a newspaper article.

Let us look at the example of one production worker. Bill has never been particularly enthusiastic about working on the production line. He worked out of duty to his wife and two small children, because he wanted to buy his own home, and because he thought dole money should go to those who couldn't get a job, not those who would simply rather not.

This year though, he applied for voluntary redundancy because he could no longer face a job which had become 'monstrous' over the last two years. But he was too late – he had been left behind in the rush.

He works two weeks of five nine-hour days, then two weeks of four nine-hour nights. He gets 20 minutes' break in the morning, 25 in the afternoon and 30 for lunch – 'just time to get indigestion, after you've queued to change a note because you've got to have the right money, and then queued again for the food'. With 4,500 workers in the body plant alone, you can imagine those queues.

He is paid a flat rate, with no bonuses and takes home about £80 a week after deductions. 'You work because you have to. No one wants to. It's a monstrous job. You can't move around. Imagine someone giving you a hammer every day and telling you to stand and tap three times, pause, tap three times. All day.

'Imagine this absolutely huge place, with everything in one colour – grey green, with all the cars going through, all grey, with no wheels or engines, in straight lines where you're not supposed to encroach on anyone else's space so you shouldn't have two people working on the same car at the same time. If you look up and see a gap in the line where there isn't a grey car, it's like heaven.'

Production lines anywhere at any time are just as bad. Management, he says, is interested only in production levels and results and to that end the men are chained to their work, treated like children, having to ask to be excused, or worse, like cheats, when after they have clocked on the foreman takes a tally later to see they are all there.

In addition to the possible human problems, large-scale production may be particularly vulnerable to changes in demand. If the firm is producing a large number of electronic typewriters and there is a revolutionary discovery which enables word processors to be sold at a quarter of their existing price, then the market for electronic typewriters is likely to fall dramatically. We have seen above how the large production run is beneficial in terms of advertising and research costs but the change in demand now means closing down a production line, which would have been very expensive to set up (the bigger you are the harder you fall). Even if the demand for such machines remains constant the large firm is more vulnerable to industrial action from small groups of key workers. It was noted above how the division of labour can improve profitability. It also means that each group of workers is reliant on others in the chain. If one group of workers goes on strike or there are production problems, the whole factory may close down. Students will be aware from reading newspapers and listening to the news that a strike of a small group of workers can close down a whole car plant.

Examination questions

1. Is a rise in the Financial Times Share Index favourable to the investor? Briefly explain your answer.

   (Q. 1(c)   1977)

2. In which financial institution would you find a bull, a bear, and a stag?

   (Q. 1(j)   1976)

3. Why may large organisations be able to produce more cheaply than small ones?

   (Q. 12   1975)

4. Name **two** of the documents which must be submitted to the Registrar of Companies when setting up a Limited Company.

   (Q. 1(a)   1980)

Public sector

Chapter 9

Two senior Conservative Cabinet Ministers said,

> 'It remains our purpose, wherever possible to transfer to the private sector, assets which can be better managed there.'
> 'It must be right to press ahead with the transfer of ownership from the state to private enterprise of as many public sector businesses as possible.'

These quotes apparently reinforce the view that many students hold, that the Conservative Party is opposed to the public sector (i.e. that part of the economy owned by the state and controlled by the government) and wishes to see everything in the private enterprise sector, while the Labour Party holds the opposite view. This is not the case. In the UK we have a mixed economy consisting of both public and private enterprise. Both parties accept this. Labour does not want to nationalise everything: the Conservatives do not wish to privatise (denationalise) everything. In *some* areas the two parties actually agree!

Areas of agreement

Some of the arguments for public ownership are accepted by all political parties.

Unprofitable services
Certain goods or services are 'essential' but they would not be provided by private enterprise because it would be unprofitable. Consider public lavatories in a seaside resort. They cost money to build and run. If they were to be profitable 'clients' might need to be charged 25p. With the sea in close proximity the public might find cheaper ways of relieving themselves! The argument of profitability also covers the

provision of parks, swimming pools and libraries. On a national level
the argument would apply to the provision of electricity. Supplying it
to large towns is profitable and private enterprise would be happy to be
involved. Supplying it to isolated villages is not, hence if it were left to
private enterprise small communities would be without electricity.

Essential services
Certain goods or services are so 'essential' to a country's well being
that they must be provided free (or almost free). Consider education
and health. A country's work-force needs to be educated and healthy.
If the provision of education and health were left to private enterprise
there might be parents too poor (or too indifferent) to be able to
educate their children properly, and sick people who might be unable
to afford treatment. The 'basics' are therefore provided by the
government (of course if you are prepared to pay, you may obtain
better education or better health treatment).

Large size and doubtful profitability
Some projects are either so enormous that no private company could
finance them or the potential profits are so dubious that private
enterprise would not be interested. The atomic energy programme is a
good example.

National security
Certain 'industries' are best controlled by the government for reasons
of national security. Atomic energy would also fall into this category as
would defence. Very few people would like to see private armies!

Areas of disagreement

A principal area of political disagreement is between those who
advocate private ownership and those who advocate public ownership
of certain enterprises.

   For example where an industry possesses numerous small firms
there may be duplication and harmful competition. If the government
organises the whole industry it can rationalise, obtain economies of
scale and therefore offer a better deal to consumers. Nonsense, say the
opponents. Competition is healthy. The inefficient go bankrupt while
only the efficient survive. Profit is the spur. If the government controls
an industry it creates a monopoly (only one firm) and because there is
no competition it can charge what it likes and be totally inefficient.
Managers become complacent because they know if there is a loss the
government will just pump in money; there is no likelihood of
bankruptcy. The pro-nationalisation lobby would deny this and claim
that monopolies exist in private enterprise and exploit the consumer. If
the monopoly is state-owned this can be avoided. Which argument you

accept depends on your political views. Thus Labour believes industries such as British Telecom, Britoil and British Airways should be part of the public sector while the Conservatives want them in the private sector.

Privatisation dispute worsens as employees are bussed in

The executive of the Post Office Engineering Union yesterday agreed to intensify its campaign to prevent the sale of British Telecom.

The union intends to black maintenance work on the telecommunications equipment of more commercial institutions. It refused to specify its targets until it has consulted with union branches, but the general secretary, Mr. Brian Stanley, said that the action would begin this week.

The union is taking industrial action against the sale of BT and the establishment of an alternative private telecommunications network, Mercury. BT management has suspended more than 2,200 union members because of the action.

When it is decided an activity should be in the public sector it will usually be run as either a nationalised industry or by the local authority.

Nationalised industries

These are known as public corporations (not to be confused with public companies which are in the private sector), are technically owned by the public and their general policy is determined by the government through the appropriate minister. The minister appoints a board to look after the day-to-day running and it submits an annual report to Parliament who (if they have time) will debate it. This is one method of public accountability; the other is through Consumer Councils who act as a watchdog on behalf of the consumer.

Phone price freeze

British Telecom said last night that it will freeze telephone charges for a year after the price increase on November 1.

The statement follows criticism from Post Office Users National Council, the consumer watchdog which monitors the Post Office and British Telecom. The Council said yesterday that the increases were not justified or necessary.

BT proposes to raise prices by an average 2.9 per cent, claiming that it cannot hold charges at present levels and also meet the Government's financial targets.

The council says the increases should be deferred until April 1984, after which there would be a year's price freeze.

The finance for nationalised industries comes from:

- revenue from the sale of its goods and services
- selling stock on the Stock Exchange
- government subsidies and grants

It is this last area that is politically most sensitive because the government subsidies come indirectly from the taxpayer and therefore mean higher taxation.

The National Coal Board yesterday offered union leaders of 190,000 mineworkers an increase on the basic rate of 5.2 per cent and told them that it was the 'last word' in the present wage bargaining round. . . . It is clear that the industry will sustain a heavy loss this financial year. . . . The main problem is that we are simply producing much more than we can sell and the over production is, in the main, from heavily losing collieries.

The opponents of public ownership claim subsidies prove the 'inefficiency' of the public sector. The validity of such an argument depends on whether such losses would still be incurred if the industry was run by the private sector. Some services (such as electricity to isolated communities) can only be provided at a loss! Any profits (and many nationalised industries are profitable) will probably go to the government to finance its spending elsewhere.

Local authorities

They provide services such as education, police, fire as well as recreational facilities. Elected councillors are responsible for broad policy but leave the day-to-day running to paid full-time employees. The finance for local authority undertakings comes from:

- revenue from the sale of services, e.g. charges to enter a swimming pool.
- grants from central government.
- local rates. Each piece of property is given a rateable value and the local authority annually fixes a rate in the pound. This is multiplied by a property's rate value and that is what the occupier pays.

Example

Rateable value	Rate in the £	Payable
200	50p	£100
300	40p	£120
400	80p	£320
500	50p	
600	25p	

● borrowing from the public. Local authorities issue fixed interest stocks which the public can buy. They are for a fixed period; on the expiration of this they must be redeemed (i.e. repaid).

Aims of public sector organisations

Organisations in the public sector do not exist solely to make profits; their political masters may use them to pursue 'political' objectives and these may conflict with the objective of profit maximisation.

Minister turns down MacGregor

Mr. Ian MacGregor, chairman of the British Steel Corporation, has advised the government to close the hot strip mill at Ravenscraig in Scotland. With over production in the industry this is essential if it is to become viable. . . . Mr. Patrick Jenkin the Secretary for Trade and Industry has insisted the mill be kept open because it is in an area of already high unemployment.

Another example would be keeping open an uneconomic coal-mine because it is in an area where there is already high unemployment.

To sum up, Table 9.1 offers a comparison of the public and private sectors.

Table 9.1   Comparison of public and private sectors

	Public sector (e.g. nationalised industries or local authorities)	Private sector (Public companies)
Sources of finance	Various, including support from government	Sale of shares to public
Control: policy	Elected representatives (e.g. Minister/Councillors)	Board of Directors
Day to day running	Paid officials (e.g. board of nationalised industry)	Senior Managers
Profits	Available to government/ local authority	Available for distribution to shareholders
Pricing	May not be able to maximise profits because of social and other objectives	Aims to maximise profitability
Responsible to	Public through their elected representatives or through Consumer Councils.	Shareholders

Examination questions

1. What is the main purpose of the Annual General Meeting of a Public Limited Liability Company?

   (Q. 1(a)   1977)

2. In terms of ownership, to whom are the Directors of a Joint-Stock company responsible?

   (Q. 1(h)   1976)

3. What special difficulties face the small private firm which wishes to expand?

   (Q. 10   1976)

4. Briefly explain the kind of information contained in:
   (i) The Memorandum;
   (ii) The Articles of Association.

   (Q. 1(d)   1975)

5. If Public Limited Companies are accountable to their shareholders, to whom are the nationalised industries accountable?

   (Q. 1(i)   1975)

6. What are the main differences between Public Limited Companies and Public Corporations?

   (Q. 10   1975)

7. Describe any **two** of the following forms of business enterprise:
   (i) The sole proprietor
   (ii) Partnerships
   (iii) Private companies
   (iv) Public Limited Liability companies

   (Q. 12   1978)

8. Consider the strengths and weaknesses of the small business unit in today's economy.

   (Q. 4   1978)

9. What are the principal ways in which business enterprises in the private sector are owned and controlled?

   (Q. 5   1973)

10. State the difference between authorised and issued capital.

    (Q. 1(c)   1983)

11. Mr Jackson has inherited £20,000. He decides to commence business as a sole trader.
    (*a*) What business problems is he likely to face?
    (*b*) Apart from retailing, in what areas might you find sole traders?

    (Q. 7   1983)

12. What is meant by limited liability?

    (Q. 1(a)   1981)

Business insurance
Chapter 10

Imagine you have just been appointed secretary to one of the managers in a large insurance company. Your manager controls a section which deals with business insurance. When you arrive at work on your first day, you are told that there is a three-day induction course. You will recall from Chapter 3 that there are three main features of an induction course. One will deal with the personal aspects of employment (information on company pay, safety, positioning of toilets, canteen, etc.), another deals with the overall picture of the company and involves describing the product or service which it provides, while the final part relates to the job the new employee is expected to perform.

Let us now consider each of these in turn.

The personal aspect
This is influenced by matters such as the layout of the building and students should revise this aspect before continuing.

The company and the service
The company which employs you supplies insurance and is therefore an **underwriter**. It is a public company and its shares are quoted on the Stock Exchange (see Table 10.1).

Table 10.1

Britannic 5p	398	Ins. Cpn. of Ireland	272 xd
Combined Int. $1	£22½	Legal & General	396
Comm. Union	154	Pearl 5p	612 xd
Eagle Star	408	Phoenix	330
Equity & Law 5p	643	Prudential	384
Gen. Accident	433	Refuge 5p	360
G.R.E.	450	Royal	530
Hambro Life 5p	352 xd	Sun Alliance £1	£11 7/8
Heath (O.E.)	320	Sun Life 5p	472
Hogg Robinson	119		

It is owned by shareholders and if the company is successful and makes a profit this will be distributed to them in the form of dividends. Not all insurance companies however are owned by shareholders. Some are owned by the **policy holders** (the people who are insured) and these are called **mutual companies.**

Having given a brief history of the company, the induction programme deals next with the nature of insurance. This is best explained by using an example.

Assume Barl Limited are a private company that manufacture small personal computers. It is a family business which started as a partnership but was formed into a private company to obtain the advantages of limited liability (in the event of bankruptcy the shareholders' liability is limited to the sum they invested in the business). The factory premises and equipment cost £100,000. The family know that it is possible, although extremely unlikely, that the factory could be burned down. As all their assets are tied up in the factory this would mean the end of the business. They therefore approach a company and ask them what the likelihood is of the factory being burned down. They are told that there is a one in ten thousand possibility. Expressed another way, the odds are ten thousand to one.

The company therefore 'bets' £10 that the company *will* be burned down. As the likelihood of this happening is ten thousand to one, the other company will agree to give them £100,000 (ten thousand times £10) in this eventuality. This pleases Barl Limited. But what about the other company (which is the insurance company)? The insurance company will offer similar odds, ten thousand to one, to all other factory owners wishing to insure against fire. Let us assume that ten thousand factory owners each pay £10 to the company. This would mean the company received £100,000. There are ten thousand businesses and given the odds of a factory burning down of one in ten thousand then only one factory will burn down. The company will receive one claim for £100,000. Thus its expenditure equals its income. Of course, in reality, an insurance company seeks to make a profit. In our example, the likelihood of a factory burning down is probably eleven thousand to one, therefore the company would receive a £110,000 from eleven thousand customers but, as only one factory is burned down, it would only pay out £100,000 leaving a surplus of £10,000. The vast majority of those taking out insurance are unable to claim and therefore lose the money they have paid in, all they get is peace of mind. Those policy holders who suffer the misfortune insured against (burglary or perhaps fire in their factory) are, however, compensated (indemnified) to the extent of their loss.

The job

The final part of the induction programme attempts to familiarise the new employee with her job. Her employer will spend a considerable amount of time out of the office and she will therefore be expected to deal with customer enquiries (these can come directly from the public or via their agents (brokers)). The enquiries can take various forms. She may receive an enquiry from a potential customer (who is referred to as the proposer) asking for details of the various policies that would be appropriate for a businessman. Her training must therefore include instruction on the various types of policies available. A list of policies and details of the cover provided can be found in Fig. 10.1.

Fig. 10.1

BUSINESS POLICIES

Basic Cover

Property

Your stock, machinery, plant, furniture, fixtures and fittings all receive essential protection against such events as fire, flood, or theft following forcible entry into or exit from the premises.

Additionally, you can cover your buildings, or, if you are a tenant, you can include in the insurance the portion of the structure and interior decorations for which you are responsible.

We will pay the cost of repair or replacement as new for your buildings or machinery.

Loss of Gross Profit

This covers you if your gross profit is reduced following interruption to your business from events covered under the Property section of this policy.

Money

Money lost or stolen from your premises, home or during transit is included. Also, if you or your employees are injured by thieves, we will pay compensation for the injury caused.

Legal Liability

If you are legally liable for injury or damage we cover your liability to
* **Your employees**
  — with no monetary limit.
* **The public**
  — up to £500,000, including your liability arising out of the sale of goods.
  In each case legal costs and expenses are also included.

Optional Covers

Glass

Accidental damage cover to your external glass, sanitaryware, neon and other fixed signs or any other glass is available.

Temporary boarding up costs are covered as well as damage to alarm foil and the removal of fixtures and fittings.

Goods in Transit

Your property can be covered against loss or damage whilst being carried in your own vehicles or despatched by road, rail or post anywhere within the British Isles.

Personal Accident

Compensation is provided for death or disablement for you and your employees following accidents at work or elsewhere.

Office Machines

Accidental damage to your office machines such as typewriters, calculators and franking machines is catered for on a full replacement basis.

Book Debts

Loss of outstanding balances due to damage to records and books of account by any event insured under the Property section is covered.

Fidelity Guarantee

You are covered for loss of money or other property following fraud or dishonesty involving any employee.

There will be other insurances which you may need according to the nature of your business.

Fig. 10.2

Commercial Union Assurance

Business Policy

Proposal Form

ASSURANCE

Agency	
Branch and Agent No.	
Policy No. UB	
Period from	to
Due date	

Please return completed proposal form to—

ASSURANCE

Commercial Union Assurance Company plc,
Registered Office: St. Helen's, 1 Undershaft, London EC3P 3DQ.
Registered in England No. 21487.

Printed for Group Supplies Department of Commercial Union Assurance

JANUARY 1982

G1729

Commercial Union Assurance Business Policy

Provides you not only with wide 'Basic' cover against fire, flood, theft and malicious damage, but also cover for those other unexpected things that can happen. Like payment for your lost gross profit if your business is unexpectedly closed or impaired, or compensation to your employees or members of the public if you are legally liable.

To this you can add a number of optional extensions to obtain the most suitable cover for your particular business needs.

For example: replacement of glass broken accidentally; compensation if you or your employees are accidentally injured or disabled whether at work or elsewhere; and payment for loss or damage to your goods in transit.

You could say it's many policies in one.

Please see the CU Business Policy prospectus and your Broker, insurance adviser or CU office for further details.

Two special advantages

Discount:
If you agree to renew your policy for three years, and the combined sums insured for Property and Loss of Gross Profit exceed £50,000, you are eligible for a 5% discount off the total premium.

Time to pay:
If you prefer, the annual premium payment for the cover you select can be spread over 5 payments by CU Credit.

CREDIT Please ask for details

Business Policy Proposal Form

Please answer questions in BLOCK CAPITALS

Full Name

Postal Address

Postcode   Telephone No.

Full description of business

      Year established

Risk address if different from above

Postcode   Telephone No.

Description of Premises e.g. store, warehouse, factory

If only part of the building is occupied by you state a) which part:

b) the nature of the business of the other occupants:

For summary of covers, please see prospectus

Basic Cover comprising:
Property, Loss of Gross Profit, Money and Liabilities insurance

Information on your business and assets — When writing in values against the various headings, please ensure they are sufficient. They should include an allowance for inflation and growth during the period to be insured; please see prospectus for guidance.

1   Buildings — the rebuilding costs including walls gates and fences plus an amount for Architects' and Surveyors' Fees, shoring up and removal of debris.   either   £

2.   Interior decorations, improvements and that portion of the structure for which you are responsible as tenant.   or   £

3.   Machinery, plant, trade and office furniture, fixtures and all other contents owned by you or your responsibility (excluding landlord's fixtures and fittings).   £

4.   Stock and materials in trade EXCLUDING jewellery, watches, furs, precious metals, precious stones, tobacco, cigars, cigarettes, non-ferrous metals and explosives.

   If any of the excluded property is to be insured, please list these separately below with sums insured applicable.

i)	£
ii)	£
iii)	£
iv)	£

5.   Estimated annual gross profit.   £

6.   Estimated wages/salaries, other than clerical, of all employees and any payments to self-employed sub-contractors:
   i)   for work at your premises   £

   ii)   for work away from your premises   £

7.   Estimated annual turnover.   £

Variations

The basic cover can be extended to meet your special requirements. Complete only if variations are required.

Loss of Gross Profit

1. If you wish to extend the indemnity period beyond 12 months to 18 months or 24 months, please indicate
   a) Period, and | Months |
   b) Estimated gross profit for this period | £ |

2. Do you wish to add loss following damage to:
   a) Surrounding property preventing access to your premises? | YES/NO |
   b) Suppliers' premises? | YES/NO |

Money

1. If you require cover in excess of £2,000 for any one loss for money in your premises during business hours, in transit or in bank night safe, please state:
   a) Amount required, and | £ |
   b) How many employees will accompany the maximum amount in transit. | [ ] |

2. If you require cover in excess of £1,000 for any one loss for money in your locked safe outside business hours, please state:
   a) Amount required, and | £ |
   b) Details of your safe, below

Make, Model and Serial Number	Is it anchored	If anchored, how?
	YES/NO	

Liability

1. Do you wish us to consider cover for exports to the U.S.A. or Canada? Please see General Question 5. | YES/NO |

Optional Covers   Please complete the sections required, otherwise leave blank

Glass

Do you require cover for:
1. External glass, comprising all fixed external glass in doors and fanlights and windows excluding glass in rooflights? | YES/NO |
2. Sanitaryware comprising fixed sinks, wash basins, lavatory pans and cisterns? | YES/NO |
3. Neon and other fixed signs? If YES, state total value. | £ |
4. Any other glass? If YES, please provide description, position and measurements.

Description	Position	Height	Width

Goods in Transit

1. **By own vehicles**
   Maximum value of goods carried at any one time. | £ |
   Number of own vehicles used for the carriage of goods. | [ ] |
2. **By other means** Please state:

	Road Hauliers	Rail	Post
Max. value of any consignment	£	£	£
Estimated annual carryings	£	£	£

Optional Covers (cont.)

Personal Accident

Name of person(s) or class of persons to be insured	Full duties of person(s) to be insured	Date(s) of birth	State number of units required (Max. of 5 units per person)

Is each person proposed to your best knowledge and belief in good health and free from physical defect? YES/NO

Office Machines – Accidental Damage

State the total value of all Office Machines to be insured. £

Describe below any item exceeding £5,000 in value or which is not within the description in the prospectus.

	£		£
	£		£
	£		£

Book Debts

Maximum amount of Outstanding Debit Balances likely to be outstanding at any one time, including a suitable allowance for expansion of business, seasonal variations, inflation and V.A.T., but deducting an allowance for bad debts. Maximum sum insured £20,000. £

Fidelity Guarantee

If NO, give details

1. Have you always been satisfied with the honesty and general conduct of all employees to be insured?

   YES/NO

2. Does your system of obtaining references and of supervision correspond to that stated in the prospectus?

   YES/NO

Other Covers

Your business could be affected in other ways.
Please indicate if you require details of the following:

Commercial vehicles or motor cars.	YES/NO
Machinery and Plant — Accidental damage, breakdown and inspection.	YES/NO
Machinery and Plant — Consequential loss.	YES/NO
Computers.	YES/NO
Cargo — Imports and exports.	YES/NO
Key people.	YES/NO

You may require additional cover for individual employees or higher limits than provided under the CU Business Policy. Do you wish to receive details for the following:

Personal Accident?	YES/NO
Fidelity Guarantee?	YES/NO

A separate proposal will need to be completed in each case.

General Questions

1. Please state
   a) whether premises are built other than of brick, stone or concrete with slate, tile, metal, asphalt or concrete roof. If YES, give details.   **YES/NO**   a)

   b) condition of repair of buildings.   b)

   c) method of heating premises if other than by
      i) low pressure, hot water or steam,
      ii) fixed electrical appliances or
      iii) fixed oil or gas fired space heaters, where the fuel is fed through fixed metal pipes and with an external flue.   c)

2. Describe:
   a) work undertaken and   a)

   b) goods supplied, installed, erected, repaired, altered or treated by you.   b)

3. Have you entered into any agreement assuming a liability for injury, illness, loss or damage for which you would not have been liable in the absence of such agreement?   **YES/NO**   If YES, please supply a copy of the agreement.

4. Do you undertake operations outside the United Kingdom? If YES, give full particulars, including countries concerned, nature of activity, wages and expenditure.   **YES/NO**

5. a) Do you import any goods?   **YES/NO**   a)

   b) Do you export any goods?   **YES/NO**   b)

   If YES, give full particulars including countries concerned. If you export to the U.S.A. or Canada state gross turnover.

   c) If you have previously exported goods to U.S.A. or Canada give full details.   c)

6. Do you supply goods for use in the nuclear, aircraft or marine industries? If YES, give full particulars including turnover. (N.B. Separate insurance may be necessary.)   **YES/NO**

7. Are any of the following used in your business? If YES, please give details.   **YES/NO**

   a) asbestos, silica, or any other substances involving a health hazard.   a)

   b) radioactive substances or other sources of ionising radiations.   b)

   c) power driven machinery.   c)

   d) flame cutting or welding plant or other heat producing plant or processes away from your own premises, by you or your sub-contractors.   d)

General Questions (cont.)

8. Are you aware of any situation where noise may be impairing hearing ability? If YES, give full details.

YES/NO

9. In connection with the insurances for which you want cover, have you:
   a) ever been refused insurance or had any special terms or conditions imposed by any Insurer?

   YES/NO

   a)

   b) during the last 3 years sustained any loss or had any claim made against you? If YES, give details.

   YES/NO

   b)

10. Are you at present insured or have you ever proposed for insurance in respect of any of the covers to which this proposal applies? If YES, state Class of Insurance and name of Insurer.

Class of Insurance	Insurer

Any other facts known to you which are likely to affect acceptance or assessment of the risks proposed for insurance must be disclosed. Should you have any doubt about what you should disclose, do not hesitate to tell us or your insurance adviser. This is for your own protection, as failure to disclose may mean that your policy will not provide you with the cover you require, or may perhaps invalidate the policy altogether.

Declaration:

I declare that the foregoing statements and particulars are true and complete and that this proposal shall form the basis of the contract with Commercial Union Assurance Company plc.

I agree to accept Insurance subject to the terms and conditions of the Company's policy and that the insurance will not be in force until the Proposal has been accepted by the Company.

Signed _____

Date _____

Space for further information if required

If the proposer is interested in one or more of the policies outlined to him, then he must be sent a **Proposal Form** (see Fig. 10.2). The information provided on this enables the company to calculate the premium (money) which the customer must pay to obtain the insurance. In the example given above, the chances of a factory burning down were quoted as ten thousand to one. In practice, the likelihood of a fire occurring will vary depending on the nature of the building and its location. A wooden building will be more likely to burn down than a brick one and a factory in the middle of a large town is at greater risk than one sited in the countryside. The more likelihood of the fire occurring the higher will be the premium.

The proposal form therefore seeks to elicit the necessary information from the proposer. The form will also ensure that the customer has an insurable interest in the property which is to be insured. This simply means that the person seeking the insurance must possess a financial interest in the risk being insured, thus the owners of the factory could insure it against fire because if it burned down they would suffer a financial loss. If a competitor tried to insure the factory there would be no insurable interest and the policy would be void. It would have no legal effect.

Having been satisfied that there is an insurable interest and once the premium has been calculated (where there is a standard policy there is a standard premium and it will not be re-calculated for each policy), the party seeking insurance can be informed of the annual premium to be paid and sent the appropriate form for payment. Although insurance policies may be paid in cash or by cheque it is more common to ask the insured party to pay by means of standing order or direct debit.

Some insurance policies have a fixed premium. This means the annual premium remains constant. A standing order would be suitable for this type of payment. If a building is being insured against fire, then the sum insured will rise every year to take inflation into account. Thus if a building is worth £100,000 and there is a 10 per cent rate of inflation, the policy would need to be increased to £110,000 the following year as this will be the sum necessary to rebuild the factory. For this reason, premiums also increase annually. A direct debit is a more suitable method of payment. It enables the bank to send varying amounts to the insurance company at the latter's request. An insurance policy needs to be 'inflation proofed' because if the sum insured is less than the value of the item you may not recover your losses.

Example:

Property worth £100,000
Insured for £75,000
Insured can only recover ¾ (100,000 ÷ 75,000) of any losses
therefore fire causes £40,000 damage
Sum recovered £30,000

Once the customer has returned the appropriate forms, the policy can be issued. In most companies it takes several days and even weeks to issue the policy. The secretary will therefore, in the meantime, issue a **cover note** to the insured. This states that the premium has been paid and the insurance cover exists. It is proof of the contract until the policy is actually issued. The latter document will contain all the terms of the contract. As stated above, most premiums are paid by means of standing order or direct debit but, where it is paid annually by cash or by cheque, the secretary will have to send out a **renewal notice** to the insured.

The final function of the secretary will be to deal with queries concerning claims. If the factory burns down Barl will wish to claim on their insurance policy. The secretary will send them a **claim form** (Fig. 10.3) and when this is returned the damage will be assessed by an Insurance company employee called an **assessor.** The extent of the loss will be calculated and this sum will be paid out by the insurance company. Although Barl have insured their building for £100,000 it may not be totally destroyed by fire. It may only have caused £70,000 of damage. As insurance compensates the policy holder for losses incurred, Barl can only claim £70,000. Once the insurance company have paid the claim they then take over the rights of the insured under the doctrine of **subrogation.** The equipment in the factory may have been severely damaged by fire and the owner compensated. The equipment then belongs to the insurance company who are entitled to sell it off as scrap. If, having been paid the value of the machinery, Barl were entitled to sell it for scrap they would then make a profit out of the insurance policy and the aim of insurance is to compensate, not to give the insured a profit. For this reason, the claim form which Barl complete will ask if the property is insured with any other insurance company. It is possible that Barl may have fire insurance with two separate companies each for £100,000. In the event of a fire causing £70,000 of damage they are not entitled to claim this sum against each insurance policy. They are entitled to only £70,000 compensation and therefore each company would pay £35,000.

Fig. 10.3

Commercial Union Assurance

Business Premises Claim Report

ASSURANCE

Please return to:

FINANCE HOUSE
          LD ROAD
          EX1 1PY

Please answer all questions on this page as fully as possible
and relevant sections on other pages.

* delete as required

Claim No._____ (Office Use Only)

Insured

Policy No._____ Renewal month_____

Insured's name_____

Address_____

_____ Postcode_____ Tel. No._____

Business_____

(a) Is the Insured registered as a taxable person? YES/NO*

(b) If the Insured is registered for V.A.T., is full remission of input tax obtained? YES/NO*

(c) If only partial remission of V.A.T. is obtained, state last annual adjusted percentage of tax recoverable _____ %

The Event

Date_____ Time_____ am/pm

When and by whom discovered_____

If known, state name and address of person causing the loss or damage_____

_____

Address where the event occurred_____

_____ Postcode_____ Tel. No._____

State rooms or area affected_____

State fully what happened_____

_____

_____

_____

_____

If illegal entry, which windows or doors were forced?_____

Were premises occupied at the time? YES/NO* If "NO" state date and time they were last occupied

Date_____ Time_____ am/pm

State date police were advised, name of station and officer's number_____

(Inform police at once if the claim is for articles lost or stolen or maliciously destroyed or damaged)

The Property Lost or Damaged

Are you the owner?   YES/NO*   If "NO" state name and address of the owner

Name and address _____

Give name(s) of any other party having an interest in the property _____

Are there any other insurances on the property?   YES/NO*

If "YES" give details (including name, address and policy no. of other insurers) _____

State total value of insured property (**Not for Glass Claims**)

Building £ _____   Stock £ _____   Other property £ _____

State nature of occupancy of premises _____

Are you responsible by agreement for the property?   YES/NO*   If "YES", please forward copy of the agreement

Have you ever before made a claim of this nature on any insurance company or underwriter?   YES/NO*

If "YES", give details: Nature of claim _____

Name of Insurers _____ Amount paid £ _____

Breakage of Glass
Details of Claim

Size _____ Type _____

Was glass sound previous to breakage?   YES/NO*

Do you require the reglazing deferred until further notice?   YES/NO*

Situation (e.g. door, window, showcase, etc) _____

Buildings (including boundary walls where specially insured)
Details of Claim

Specify separately each room or building damaged or destroyed and how occupied	Age of building or damaged fixtures/ fittings, water tanks, etc.	Date when last decorated (each room or part damaged)	Amount of tradesman's estimate **Please attach estimate**	Adjustment for previous depreciation alterations or improvements	Net amount of claim
			£		£

If necessary continue on a separate sheet

Contents
Details of Claim

(mark an X in the last column if articles are on loan, hire or belong to a customer)

Description of articles (attach estimates for articles repairable)	From whom obtained (name and address)	Date acquired or manu-factured	Cost (net of profit & V.A.T.) price	Value of salvage	Net amount of claim less deprec-iation, salvage, profit & V.A.T., etc.	V.A.T. if claimed
			£	£	£	£

If necessary continue on a separate sheet

Property in the open

Describe fully and state situation	From whom obtained (name and address)	Date acquired or manu- factured	Cost (net of profit & V.A.T.) price	Value of salvage	Net amount of claim less deprec- iation, salvage, profit & V.A.T., etc.	V.A.T. if claimed
			£	£	£	£

Contract Works

State form of Contract (e.g. R.I.B.A., I.C.E., etc.) _____

Any special terms?   YES/NO*

Period of contract from _____ to _____

State value of whole contract   £ _____

Declaration

I declare that these particulars are true to the best of my knowledge.

Signature _____   Date _____

Commercial Union Assurance Company plc, Registered Office: St. Helen's, 1 Undershaft, London EC3P 3DQ. Registered in England No. 21487
Printed by Group Supply Department of Commercial Union Assurance.

FEBRUARY 1981

GSF769(d)

Examination questions

1. Why is an insurance company better able to afford risks than is a firm seeking insurance cover? Give two examples of insurance cover a firm might seek.
   (Q. 4   1976)   *(Q. 4   1976)*

2. What is meant by an insurable risk?
   (Q. 1(h)   1975)   *(Q.1(h)   1975)*

3. What are the main principles underlying insurance agreements?
                                                                                                       (Q. 11   1975)

4. Imagine you are an insurance agent trying to 'sell insurance' to a small business. Explain the main insurances you would recommend and the reasons why you think they are needed by this business.
                                                                                                       (Q. 6   1978)

5. What are the chief risks that the owners of a small factory might insure against?
                                                                                                       (Q. 10   1974)

6. As part of an internal training course an insurance firm is providing a list containing definitions of insurance terms. Suggest suitable definitions for the following words: proposer, premium, cover note, subrogation, fidelity guarantee.
                                                                                                       (Q. 3   1983)

The government and the economy

Chapter 11

Of what relevance is this topic to the potential secretary? In the first place it may affect her employer.

Imagine you are a secretary employed by a firm manufacturing electronic typewriters. How would your employers be affected by:

1. An import tariff on electronic goods?
2. An increase in domestic interest rates?
3. A strong domestic currency?

If there is an import tariff (tax) on electronic goods this will increase the price of imported electronic typewriters. This would improve the sales of your firm because your competitors' machines are now more expensive. You are working for a more profitable firm and are therefore less likely to be made redundant and more likely to receive a pay increase. If there are high interest rates this will have the opposite effect on the profits of your employers. They would almost certainly have borrowed money to start up in business and will now have to pay higher interest on this. In addition the higher interest rates may discourage firms from investing in new equipment and this could mean reduced sales for your employers. If your firm is making less profit it will need less staff; your job could be at risk. Finally, if the domestic currency is strong this will make imported goods cheaper and it will make the goods you sell more expensive to foreigners. There is more competition on the home market and it will be more difficult to export. This could mean fewer sales for your firm with the unpleasant consequences that will follow.

Just as the decisions which the government makes may affect your future employer, it may also affect you as an individual.

Suppose that you intend to buy a Japanese car on hire purchase. How would you be affected by:

1. An import quota on Japanese cars;
2. The tightening up of hire purchase restrictions?

If there is a restriction on the number of Japanese cars that can be imported you may well find it difficult to buy a model and because they are scarce the price may rise. The tightening of hire purchase restrictions may mean that instead of putting down a deposit of say 10 per cent of the cost of the car, you may be required to put down a 20 per cent deposit. The effect of both of these may mean that you are unable to purchase the car you wanted.

When the government gets involved in the economy it affects you. Why does the government get involved?

Provision of services

The government has to provide certain services and it needs the money to pay for these and Table 11.1 gives an indication of how the government spends its money.

Table 11.1 Government expenditure

	Expenditure (£ billion)	Percentage
Defence	17·0	13
Education	12·6	10
Social Security	37·2	30
Social Services	15·4	12
Law and Order	4·9	4
Housing	2·5	2
Roads	4·4	3
Miscellaneous	30·0	26

The amount spent will vary depending on the political party which happens to be in power. Some parties believe in considerable state involvement in the economy while others believe that the state should only be involved in providing the minimum of services. It is important to appreciate that no political party has ever claimed that no services should be provided by the government. Some services are so crucial that they cannot be left to private enterprise; for instance, one of the largest elements of expenditure is defence and all parties agree that it is the responsibility of the state to pay for this. Again, there is political agreement that education, social services and the police should all be provided for by the state, although there may be disputes as to the amount of private enterprise that should be allowed in these areas.

Given the need to provide these services the government must raise sufficient funds to pay for them. It can do this in two ways:

Taxation

Finance can be raised by levying direct or indirect taxes on the citizens or the companies within a country. Direct taxes are collected by the Inland Revenue and are levied directly on the individual or the company that has to pay them. They include income tax and corporation tax. Thus income tax is paid directly (which is why it is called a direct tax) by the taxpayer to the Inland Revenue. It is deducted from your wage packet by your employer.

Indirect taxes are collected by the Customs and Excise and, unlike direct taxes, they are not collected directly from the taxpayer. Thus VAT, which is an indirect tax, is levied on goods or services. The consumer buying a washing machine may pay £150; of this £120 may go to the retailer and £30 may be destined for the tax man. The consumer is not really concerned with this, but is mainly interested in the purchase price, £150. Once the retailer has collected the money he remits the appropriate amount to the Customs and Excise. The consumer is therefore paying the tax indirectly.

Taxation is not, however, used solely to raise revenue. It can be used by the Chancellor of the Exchequer to achieve social or political aims. Consider how the Chancellor could use taxation to:

1. discourage smoking
2. encourage firms to adopt new technology
3. re-distribute income from the wealthy to the poorer groups within society
4. affect the retail price index

(The answers can be found at the end of the chapter.)

Borrowing

Where government expenditure exceeds the revenue obtained from taxes then the deficit must be made up by borrowing.

The choice of where to raise revenue and how much should be raised has both political and economic implications. Suppose you are the Chancellor of the Exchequer and you calculate government expenditure will be £100,000,000 but you decide to collect only £90,000,000 in taxes and to finance the other expenditure by borrowing £10,000,000. What effect will this have on the economy? As can be seen in Fig. 11.1 the government expenditure of £100,000,000 ultimately finds its way back to the consumer in the form of wages and dividends. The public therefore have £100,000,000 to spend but they have had to pay out only £90,000,000 in taxes. The net result therefore is that there is an additional £10,00,000 to buy goods and services (the public have lost £90m. but gained £100m.). This may well have the effect of stimulating the domestic (home) economy. The consumer has more money to spend and therefore will require more goods. If she buys home manufactured products then in order to produce these the manufacturers will have to purchase more equipment and take on additional labour; this reduces unemployment. The additional labour will be paid and they will use this money to purchase more goods, this in turn will create further employment. When a Chancellor therefore wishes to stimulate (expand) the economy he may well decide to bring in a deficit budget, which is the technical name used when his expenditure exceeds the amount of revenue he raises from taxation.

Fig. 11.1

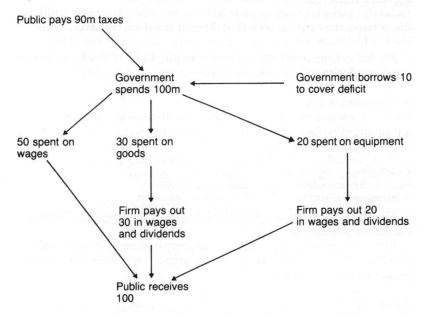

Economic objectives

The government wants to obtain the economic objectives that it has been elected to achieve.

Although the policies which political parties may follow vary, most parties seek to obtain four main objectives.

1. Full employment
This does not mean that everybody must have a job but merely that the rate of unemployment falls within an acceptable figure. What is acceptable will depend on the political party.

2. Low inflation figures
This is an essential prerequisite of some of the other objectives. A high domestic inflation rate can affect a country's competitiveness in overseas markets and have a damaging effect on the balance of payments. Given an exchange rate of £1 = 10 francs consider the following:

Cost of car in UK £5,000
Cost of car in France 50,000 fr.

Financially it makes no difference whether the UK citizen buys a car here or in France. Suppose:

Inflation in UK 10 per cent
Inflation in France 5 per cent
Cost of UK car £5,000 + 10 per cent = £5,500
Cost of French car 50,000 + 2,500 = 52,500 which at £1 = 10 francs means it will cost
52,500 ÷ 10 = £5,250

The UK citizen now finds it cheaper to purchase a French car, hence imports will rise and the balance of payments will deteriorate.

3. Economic growth
It is a natural human reaction to want to be better off. This is not automatically achieved by higher wages as the increase may be offset by the rise in inflation.

Example:
Salary £5,000 Expenditure on food, heating, etc. £5,000
Salary increase 10 per cent = £5,500 Prices rise by 10 per cent

Therefore salary buys same amount of food, heating, etc. The wage earner is no better off.

Economic growth means that the country is producing more and therefore there is more to go round. Everybody may therefore have a higher standard of living.

Example:
Salary £5,000 Expenditure on food, heating, etc. £5,000
Salary increase 5 per cent = £5,250 Inflation 1 per cent = £50

Therefore the wage earner only needs £5,050 to buy equivalent amount of food, heating, etc. She has £200 remaining to purchase additional items and is therefore better off. Your standard of living only rises if wages increase faster than inflation.

4. A stable balance of payments
This is a prerequisite of achieving the others. If the balance of payments falls into deficit and the country is forced to borrow or draw on its reserves, then it may be forced to take remedial action to improve the balance of payments. This could have a detrimental effect on its economic growth and levels of employment.

Obtaining economic objectives

To obtain the objectives detailed above the government may use: fiscal policy; devaluation; high interest rates.

1. Fiscal policy (taxation)
One already mentioned would be a budget deficit (see Fig. 11.1 on page 112).

Fig. 11.2

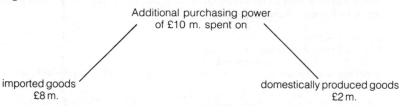

Additional purchasing power
of £10 m. spent on

imported goods   domestically produced goods
£8 m.   £2 m.

The budget deficit results in an increase in purchasing power within the community. If this increased purchasing power is spent on domestically produced goods there will be an increased demand for labour and a reduction in the unemployment figures. As Fig. 11.2 indicates, however, part of the additional spending power may be spent on imports. This may then lead to a balance of payments problem. As we saw in Chapter 6 this may result in a weakening of the domestic currency. If this happens it makes imported goods more expensive and where a country imports raw materials or foodstuffs this will result in higher prices for the consumer and inflation. Even if this does not occur and all the increased purchasing power is spent on domestic goods, a time may arise when there is insufficient productive capacity at home to meet the demand. This will mean imports will be purchased and the demand for domestic products will force their prices up, again resulting in inflation. A budget deficit may therefore achieve economic growth and full employment while at the same time causing inflation and an unstable balance of payments.

2. Devaluation
From Fig. 11.3 it can be seen that following a devaluation the domestic currency will be worth less in terms of other currencies, thus instead of £1 being worth 10 francs, £1 would only buy 8 francs. The reader will remember from the chapter on international trade (Ch. 6) that as a consequence of a devaluation exports will rise because domestic goods will be cheaper to foreigners (in our example British goods will be cheaper in France). At the same time because the domestic currency will buy less foreign currency, foreign goods become more expensive. It therefore follows that imports should fall. Given that exports rise and imports fall there will be a balance of payments surplus and an increased demand for British goods both here (because the goods of foreign competitors are now more expensive) and from abroad. This will necessitate an increase in production to meet the increased demand which should result in additional workers being required. Thus the devaluation should achieve a balance of payments surplus, less unemployment and economic growth.

There is a problem, however. As we have seen above, imports become more expensive and we have therefore assumed that people no longer buy them and turn to British produced goods. In some cases,

Fig. 11.3

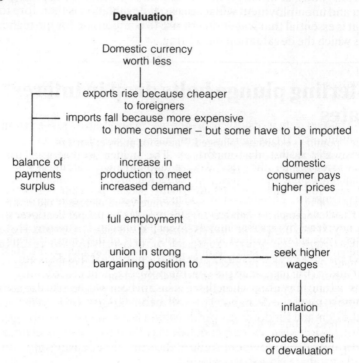

Devaluation
|
Domestic currency
worth less
|
exports rise because cheaper
to foreigners
imports fall because more expensive
to home consumer – but some have to be imported

balance of
payments
surplus

increase in
production to meet
increased demand

domestic
consumer pays
higher prices

full employment

union in strong
bargaining position to

seek higher
wages

inflation

erodes benefit
of devaluation

however, this will not be possible. Britain, like most countries, lacks certain raw materials and is forced to import these. In addition, certain foreign products may not be produced in this country or may be so popular that people still require them, even though the cost has risen. The cost of importing foreign goods has risen and this will be reflected in the prices which retailers charge in the shops. It follows that the domestic consumer will therefore be forced to pay higher prices, and in consequence is likely to seek higher wages. As was seen in Chapter 1 this is one of the functions of the union and because there is full employment, the union will be in a strong bargaining position. Employers will be anxious to recruit staff to cope with the increased demand and are more likely therefore to agree to higher wage demands rather than risk damaging strikes. Because the demand for goods is high they will feel confident that they can pass on the higher wage costs to the consumer in the form of higher prices. This of course will lead to inflation. As domestic prices increase so the value of the devaluation will lessen (as explained above) and a point will eventually be reached where British goods are more expensive than imported goods, at which point the balance of payments will go into deficit and unemployment will increase. If devaluation is therefore to work it is essential that wages do not rise to compensate for the higher prices which the devaluation must bring.

Sterling plunge halts drop in interest rates

The pound yesterday plunged downwards against most important currencies for the third day running, wiping out hopes that interest rates will start falling again soon . . .

The Government is standing by to intervene by raising interest rates if the snowball effect in the foreign exchange markets gets out of hand. But it has so far accepted an overall devaluation of sterling approaching 4 per cent in the last three days . . .

The decline threatens to raise retail prices, but it will be good news for many exporters. . . . .

The sudden weakness of the pound threatens to reinject some inflation into the economy, because each 1 per cent fall in its average value increases the retail price index by 0.3 per cent over a year. Whitehall is stressing that only a part of this comes through quickly, in prices such as oil. But with a 3.8 per cent fall in sterling's average value this week, more than 1 per cent will be added to the RPI [Retail Price Index] over a year.

---

3. High interest rates (Fig. 11.4)
If there are high interest rates, then foreigners will wish to invest their money in the UK to take advantage of these (as explained on page 76). There will be a healthy demand for sterling and the £ will be 'strong'. This means the opposite of devaluation. Thus instead of an Englishman obtaining 10 francs for £1 he will obtain 12 francs. It follows from this that British goods will be expensive to foreigners while the price of foreign goods (imports) will be cheaper. This means that manufacturers will pay lower prices for their raw materials, hence price rises should be kept to a minimum. This will therefore achieve a low inflation rate. Given however that it makes exporting difficult and reduces the price of imports, it is likely to have an adverse effect on the balance of payments. In addition there will be a lack of demand for UK goods both at home (because we will import goods) and abroad (because they will be more expensive than those of our competitors). As a consequence, British firms are likely to produce less. The decision to produce less is reinforced by the high interest rates which makes it very expensive for industry to borrow money to re-equip or to carry stocks of goods. If a firm produces goods which are not sold it must carry them in the warehouse and if the goods are worth, say, £1,000,000 then it has this sum of money tied up. If interest rates are 15 per cent the cost of tying up £1,000,000 in stock is £150,000.

Fig. 11.4

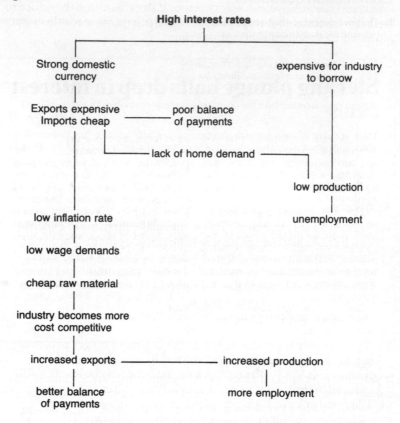

Manufacturers will therefore reduce production and this results in unemployment. Clearly, then, three of the objectives, balance of payments, employment and economic growth, are not achieved in the short term. In the long term, the low inflation rate caused by the strong currency should result in lower wage demands. Industry therefore has the benefit of low cost for raw materials and lower wage rises than its competitors. It is anticipated that this should make industry more efficient. As it becomes more efficient it is therefore able to sell its goods overseas which improves the balance of payments and to increase domestic sales at the expense of imports. The net result of the increased sales both at home and abroad should lead to full employment. If the objectives are therefore to be achieved through a strong domestic currency, it is crucial that British industry takes advantage of the low cost to become more efficient vis à vis the rest of the world.

Examination questions

1. The government controls the economy in a variety of ways. Distinguish by examples between fiscal and monetary policy.

   (Q. 1(i)   1977)

2. Give: (i) **one** example of a direct tax; and
   (ii) **one** example of an indirect tax.

   (Q. 1(d)   1976)

3. Name a reason (other than the raising of government revenue) why tax is levied.

   (Q. 1(c)   1975)

4. There are various ways in which governments can fight inflation. Explain the way in which your government has attempted to reduce inflation or maintain it at a low rate.

   (Q. 10   1982)

Answers

1. Raise VAT on cigarettes. This would make them more expensive which might discourage people from smoking them. The tax of course will generate income. A Chancellor who wanted 'energy saving' measures to be introduced into houses might 'encourage' householders by taxing gas, oil and coal. This would provide an incentive to reduce consumption.

2. Give grants to firms or agree to waive corporation tax on the profits for one year.

3. A progressive tax (i.e. one where the rich pay a bigger percentage of their income than the poor) is one way of achieving this.

4. A change in VAT will affect prices and hence the index. If VAT is reduced by 5 per cent prices will fall. If it is increased the index rises. The retail price index is one factor influencing wage demands. The higher it is the bigger increase the unions will claim. If the government wishes to raise revenue but does not wish to see the index rise it will increase the rate of income tax. Although an employee's take home pay (salary less deductions such as tax and national insurance) is reduced, prices will not rise.

Section B

Starting up
Chapter 12

Dennis Kay is the South Western Sales Manager for an organisation supplying office equipment. The company wish to move him to the North East, but because he and his family are happy living in Devon, he decides to resign and set up in business on his own account. Given his business background, he is considering opening a shop in Plymouth. He employs a market research firm to conduct a survey into consumer needs. The questionnaire they devise produces a positive response and he therefore decides to go ahead.

To establish himself in business he will require premises, but before he can look for these he must make arrangements to obtain the necessary finance.

Finance

Given that Kay is setting up on his own account, he will be a sole trader and you will remember that he has to provide the finance himself, either from his own resources or by borrowing the money from friends or the bank. If he chooses to take somebody else into the business as a partner, then the capital must be found by the partners (a public company would be able to raise funds by issuing shares to the public up to the value of its authorised capital). Once he is satisfied that he has sufficient capital to start the business, Kay will need to find premises.

Premises

In order to purchase premises Kay decides to take out a mortgage. This is a loan but differs from a bank loan in that it will be for a long period, often up to 25 years. He can obtain the mortgage from a building society, such as the Halifax, or one of the commercial banks, such as the Midland or the National Westminster. The security (collateral) for the mortgage is the property to be purchased. In the event of Kay being unable to make the mortgage repayments, the building society or bank will be able to sell the property and use the funds obtained to pay off the loan, any surplus being given to Kay. The legal formalities involved in the purchase will be dealt with by Kay's solicitor and the purchase will be completed when the solicitor hands over the banker's draft (cheque drawn upon the bank) for the appropriate sum.

Having purchased his premises, Kay will need to engage and train his staff.

Staff

The recruitment of staff in a large company would be the function of a Personnel Department. They would arrange for the appropriate advertisement to be placed in a local newspaper, for the application forms to be sent out to interested parties and for the selection interviews to be held. In a small company it is not possible to have specialist managers and so these functions will be performed by Kay.

He decides to start with a staff of two. Once the staff are engaged he will then have to organise their training programme. He intends to offer a word processing service to small firms and therefore both his staff need to be competent on the Xerox word processor he has purchased. There are short word processing courses at the local College of Further Education. Should he send the staff on these? The answer is, almost certainly, no. It is important that his staff learn how to operate a Xerox word processor, whereas those in the local college are Bitsy Secretaires. Manufacturers, aware of the training problems, will undertake when they sell a word processor to train one or two operators free of charge before the machine arrives, or immediately on its delivery. It is therefore, almost certain that the company delivering the Xerox word processor will arrange for the staff to be trained.

Once the word processor is installed what happens if a member of staff who has been trained leaves? What is the most appropriate method for teaching her replacement how to use the machine? A college course is out, for the reason outlined above, and letting her learn by sitting next to the other operator is not desirable for a number of reasons. Firstly, the other employee although a competent operator, may be a poor teacher and unable to teach her the proper skills and if she has developed any bad habits these will be transferred to the new employee. Secondly, the word processor will be in use and it will not therefore be possible to plan the teaching so that the new employee is taken through the procedures step by step. In addition, the pressures within a busy office may not be conducive to learning. For these reasons it will be better if a new employee receives off-the-job training away from the normal working environment. She may therefore be sent on a course organised by the manufacturers of the machine.

It may however have been possible to recruit a new member of staff who already has the necessary skills. She may have attended a full-time course at the College of Further Education where, although she may have learned on another machine, she will have the basic word processing skills and should be able to transfer these relatively easily by reading the manual and talking to the experienced operator. Or the new employee might have received instruction through one of the courses organised by the Manpower Services Commission. This may have been a course for mature applicants or one of the courses designed for unemployed school-leavers, which consists of a period of training supplemented by a period of work experience.

Kay also wishes to train both his new staff on the switchboard. Given that both have a suitable telephone technique, this type of training is probably best done on the job and given to employees in the normal working situation. The employee to be trained will sit next to somebody who can use the switchboard, watch her and then use the switchboard under her supervision. Once she is competent she will then be allowed to work on her own.

If the business expands Kay may wish one of his staff to undertake more accountancy work. In order to acquire the necessary skills she may be sent away to the local college on a day-release scheme to take the examinations of one of the accountancy bodies.

The engagement and training of staff are two of the personnel functions which Kay must perform. He will also have to perform one of the functions of the Accounts Department, the calculation and payment of staff wages. From their gross wages, sums will be deducted for National Insurance and income tax (which you will recall is a direct tax) and the remaining sum will be paid to the employees. If they agree, this sum will be paid directly into their current accounts at the bank. They can then draw out any sums they require by writing out cheques or using their cash cards.

Only one thing remains to be done before Kay can set up in business and that is to buy the equipment.

Equipment

The equipment which Kay requires (word processors, computers, photocopiers etc) is expensive. A word processor, for example, might cost £6,000. Once it has been purchased and installed it may generate an income of £100 per week; this means that it will take approximately 60 weeks before Kay has recovered the initial cost. He may be able to finance their purchase from the capital which he or his partners initially contributed, alternatively he may approach his bank for a short-term loan (the income produced from the equipment purchased should be enough to repay the loan within two years). Before giving him the loan the bank will require collateral (security). This may be the equipment purchased or anything else which the bank could sell in the event of Kay failing to repay the loan on time.

Instead of seeking a bank loan, Kay may decide to purchase the equipment on credit. With hire purchase he would pay a deposit on the item and then agree to pay the balance, plus interest, over a fixed period. The advantage of this scheme would be that the machines would produce sufficient income to cover the monthly instalments. When the final instalments have been paid Kay would become the legal owner of the goods. Until that point they will remain the property of the sellers who can, with the court's permission, re-possess them if Kay fails to pay his instalments.

Kay can now start trading once he has taken out the necessary insurance policies.

Let us assume that Kay's business has expanded and he is now writing and developing computer programmes. Being based in Plymouth he is also considering exporting these to France, especially as the pound is weak against the franc. The computer expansion is costly because it involves new premises and equipment and exporting to France means establishing premises there. Kay requires additional finance.

A large public company could raise additional long-term capital by issuing shares to the public. However, the cost of becoming a public company is considerable and it is uneconomic to raise less than £500,000 in a share issue. Kay must obviously look to other sources of finance.

He has already had an overdraft from his bank to pay bills when he was starting up and the bank manager is now prepared to offer him a loan. Unfortunately this will only provide short-term finance whereas Kay needs finance for a longer period.

It is possible that retained profits could be used but in Kay's case these have already been re-invested in the business. He therefore approaches a merchant bank. Unlike the commercial banks (those you see in the High Street) which deal with both the public and businesses, merchant banks deal only with businesses.

He may be successful in obtaining funds from the merchant bank because they specialise in providing 'venture capital'. This is money invested in a small business which has little collateral but where the potential profits are considerable (as in the case with the 'new technology'). In return for the investment the bank obtains part of the business. Although the investment is risky one success will offset numerous failures.

Not only will the merchant bank provide capital, it will also advise Kay on potential export problems. It will advise him on the currency situation, exchange controls and problems of insurance.

Saving for a house
Chapter 13

Most people hope at some time to be able to buy their own house, and the sources of finance to would-be house-owners have been described earlier. It was also remarked that the banks or building societies would not provide a mortgage for the whole of the purchase price. It is normally a percentage of the valuation and this is usually less than the purchase price. You may be buying a house for £30,000 but it is likely that the building society surveyor will put a valuation on it of say £28,000, leaving the would-be purchaser to find £2,000, as well as the legal fees and the cost of the surveyor's report. Before embarking on house purchase, therefore, you will need to have saved several thousand pounds.

Being aware of this, you and your fianceé or husband decide to save £20 per week from your salaries. In less than three years' time you will have saved £3,000. You allocate £2,000 for the deposit and £1,000 for other costs. This, of course, pre-supposes that the property you are after will still cost £30,000 in three years' time. It is likely, however, that house prices will rise in the next three years because of inflation.

If there is 10 per cent inflation, then

Year 1 £30,000 plus 10% = £33,000
Year 2 £33,000 plus 10% = £36.300
Year 3 £36,300 plus 10% = £39,630

The amount saved, £3,000, was to be 10% of the purchase price (£30,000). Given inflation, at the end of the three years the sum required has risen to £3,963. If your savings had been left in a **current account** on which no interest was paid, then you would have to save an additional £963. It is therefore crucial that when you save money it is invested so that it will increase in line with inflation.

One possibility is to ask your bank to open a **deposit account.** You could arrange for your bank to transfer £20 a week automatically from your current to your deposit account, where it will earn interest. Some banks will guarantee its depositors a mortgage. The capital in the deposit account is secure, but the interest payable may be below the rate of inflation.

Alternatively, it may be decided to open an account with a building society. This is similar to a deposit account in that interest is paid and the capital is secure. It also gives depositors priority when seeking a mortgage. There are different types of accounts with building societies but it would be unwise to select one which involved leaving the savings untouched for a period of years as you may require the money before the end of this period if a suitable house is found.

The choice of bank or building society could therefore depend on which offers the higher rate of interest. The rate quoted by the banks always looks higher because it is quoted before tax, whereas the rate quoted by the building societies is net of tax. What this means is that when you receive interest from the building society you do not have to pay tax on it, but the sums paid by the banks must be declared to the tax authorities and tax paid. Thus:

Deposit account at bank 8% (gross) Oct. 1983
Interest rate at building society 7¾% (net) 11% (gross) Oct. 1983

The bank figure is a gross figure (although this may not always be clear). The building society will quote a figure net of tax, but it will also quote a gross interest rate. It is this figure which should be compared with the rate offered by the banks.[1]

As stated above, both of these investments are secure, but if the rate of inflation is 10 per cent and the interest you receive (after tax has been paid) is 5 per cent, then it follows that your capital is not increasing as fast as the rate of inflation.

In an attempt to find an investment which will rise faster than the rate of inflation you may be tempted to look at **stocks and shares.** The **Financial Times Share Index** (which monitors the general progress of stocks and shares) will rise over the long term to compensate for the rate of inflation. Inflation merely reflects the rise in prices. If there is high inflation, it means that companies are charging higher prices to the consumers and this should ultimately be reflected in increased profits for the company resulting in higher share prices. The difficulty for the investor is that, although this is a long-term trend, there are times when the **Financial Times Index** may actually fall, although prices are rising. If you are buying a house then you may wish to sell your shares (realise your assets) at a time when share prices are actually falling. You may find that the £1,000 you invested is now only worth £900. Of course, if share prices are rising, the investment might be worth £1,200. A further complication for the small investor is that shares in individual companies may not follow the general trend of share prices. Thus the **Financial Times Index** may be increasing but the shares of British Leyland may be falling because there is a serious industrial

[1] The situation is being changed in 1985 to bring banks into line with building societies.

stoppage at BL which has brought production to a standstill. Conversely, a successful introduction of a new car might cause the share price to rise although the FT Index is static or even falling. Interest, of course, is not paid on shares (the shareholders receive dividends which depend on companies' profits) but the main reason for not investing funds in stocks and shares is the risk involved. You may however decide at the end of one year to leave £800 of your savings in the deposit account or with the building society and to invest £200 in shares, hoping that you may make a speculative gain.

Rather than selecting an individual company you might choose to invest in a **Unit Trust.** This means giving the funds to an investment manager in return for units in the Trust. You will own not shares in companies but part of the trust. The investment manager will then invest the funds in a variety of shares. The total value of all the investments will determine the value of the fund and therefore the value of the units held. The investment manager is a specialist who will buy and sell shares on behalf of the fund in an attempt to make a capital gain (profit) for the unit holders. By entrusting the funds to a specialist who can invest them over many securities it is therefore hoped to minimise the risk.

Example

A trust has 1,000,000 investors each contributing £10.
£10 = 1 unit
Trust Capital £10,000,000
Invested in 1,000,000 shares, current value £10,000,000
Each unit holder owns $\frac{1}{1,000,000}$ of the trust.
Shares owned increase in value to £15,000,000
Each unit held now is worth £15 ($\frac{1}{1000,000}$ of £15,000,000)

It is also possible to invest money in **gilt-edge securities.** These are issued by the government for a fixed period of time and because the government guarantees them, there is no possibility of investors losing all their money (unlike stocks in companies where, if they go bankrupt, investors do lose their money). They are therefore a more secure investment than ordinary shares, but their value can change. To understand this, let us assume that the government has issued a number of certificates and has promised that it will pay the holder of each certificate £5 interest annually. If I pay £100 for one of these certificates then the rate of interest payable is 5 per cent (£5 on the £100 investment). Like stocks and shares these certificates can be traded on the Stock Exchange so that investors may realise their assets. Let us now assume that interest rates have risen to 10 per cent; the holder of one of these certificates will still only receive £5. A prospective purchaser will only be willing to buy the certificate if the interest (£5) is equivalent to 10 per cent of the sum he invests, i.e. the price he pays for the share. It therefore follows that he would only be prepared to pay

£50 for the certificate, (£5 is 10 per cent of £50). If interest rates rise therefore the value of gilt-edge securities on the stock market will fall. Conversely, if interest rates fall then the value of gilt-edge securities will rise. If interest rates were to fall to 2½ per cent, then the holder of a certificate would expect to sell it at £200 because £5 paid on a £200 investment is 2½ per cent.

You will appreciate that the value of gilt-edge securities depends on the movement of interest rates, therefore investing in gilt edge securities is best left to the experts.

An industrial dispute

Chapter 14

A multi-national car firm manufacturing cars in the UK is in the process of automating its production line using robots. It hopes that this will produce cost savings which will enable it to compete more effectively. It is particularly concerned about overseas competition as there is a strong pound which has made it more difficult to export, while at the same time making imported cars cheaper to the domestic purchaser. The sales at home and abroad have therefore fallen and coupled with the growing use of robots, the company needs fewer employees. The need to reduce the wages bill is made more urgent because the company has a large overdraft at the bank and interest rates are at present very high (this is one of the reasons why there is a strong pound).

As a result of the falling profits the Board of Directors have instructed the Personnel Director to put the staff on to short-time working. This means that the employees will work only four days a week. The Personnel Director decides to inform staff by putting notices on the notice board and into all the pay packets stating simply, 'As from Monday 14th, all staff will work a four-day week and the factory will be closed on Fridays'. Within one hour of these notices being read the shop stewards ask to see the Personnel Director.

In communicating this information to the staff he has made several serious mistakes.

(a) What he has said is incomplete. There has been no attempt to explain to the staff the reason for the decision.

(b) He has chosen an inappropriate method of communicating his message. Both the notice board and the written notice to the staff are one-way communications. They do not enable the staff to ask questions to clarify any points of confusion. As a result of defects within the formal channels of communication the informal channels (the grapevine) have taken over. The problem with these, as far as

management are concerned, is that they have no control over the information being passed down. In this situation one member of staff, having seen the notice, has assumed that this is a prelude to staff being made redundant (losing their jobs). He has communicated this fear to a colleague and within minutes the work-force are talking about redundancies. To make matters worse the rumour has spread that the reason for these redundancies is that the firm is transferring production of one of the models to a new factory that it is building in Spain.

(c) The union are upset because the Personnel Director has not gone through the formal channels of communication. Within any organisation there are formal channels and where people are bypassed they are likely to resent this as they may believe it implies a loss of status. The shop stewards are concerned because the Personnel Director has chosen to go directly to the staff over their heads. They are convinced he had some ulterior motive for doing this.

There is a meeting of the Joint Shop Stewards' Committee which consists of the shop stewards from the three main unions involved in the plant. There is a white-collar union representing the managerial and clerical staff. A craft union representing a small group of electricians and the general union (which is the largest) representing 80 per cent of the employees. The committee has elected a Chief Shop Steward who can act as a spokesman for all the unions. The demands of the committee, which includes no short-time working, are put to the Personnel Director who rejects them.

Following the unsatisfactory meeting with the management the committee meets again to decide on the action to take. They consider a work-to-rule and a strike. As the effect of both of these will be to reduce the number of cars produced they reject them, feeling this would be playing into the hands of management. As they consider the issues involved to be extremely serious, however, they recommend to their members that the local branch should refer the matter to the Regional Committee with a recommendation that if the Regional Officers cannot obtain a satisfactory response from the management, the matter should be referred to the National Executive. Following further fruitless negotiations this is eventually done. The National Executive Committee is responsible for putting union policies into practice and it is headed by the union's senior full-time official, the General Secretary. The Executive discusses the problem of the car workers and decides that there are both short-term and long-term problems involved. The short-term problem is how to avoid any redundancies or short-time working. They therefore instruct the General Secretary to inform the firm's management that if there are any redundancies or short-term working, they will organise a strike at the car firm's other UK plant. This is working at full capacity producing a new model which has captured a large share of the UK market. The union realise that if production of this plant is halted it will have a disastrous effect on the firm's profitability. To stop the car firm (which is multi-national) switching its production to plants overseas, the General Secretary is instructed to have talks with union colleagues in other countries to gain their support. Such talks have already been held on other issues as indicated by the following article:

Fight for car jobs to cross borders

Union leaders representing more than 100,000 Ford workers throughout Europe have pledged to fight the company's rationalisation plans.

A three-day meeting in Valencia ended on Sunday with a promise of "international solidarity by Ford workers to prevent one group of Ford workers in one country being played off against another".

The meeting, which was attended by representatives from seven countries, also promised "to resist any attempts by the company to improve the status of Ford's Japanese partner, Toyo Kogyo, at the expense of Ford's existing operations". . . .

Steve Broadhead, convener at the strike-hit Halewood body plant, attended the meeting and said yesterday: "It became apparent during our discussions that the company's claim that other plants in other countries have accepted Japanese-style working practices is simply not true." . . .

The Ford UK delegation, led by Dagenham convener Bernie Passingham, promised to support their Belgian colleagues, who today begin annual pay negotiations. Last year Belgian Ford workers narrowly voted against a strike in pursuit of a 39-hour week.

The long-term problem is to improve the competitiveness of UK industry. Because this involves many unions, the Executive asks each General Secretary to bring it up at the appropriate committee of the Trade Union Congress. At this committee the whole matter is discussed and the TUC decides to make representations to the government to modify their economic strategy. In particular, they request:

1. A reduction in interest rates. This will have the two-fold effect of reducing the operating cost of UK industry and weakening the pound (because foreigners will no longer wish to deposit their money in the UK) which will result in exports being made cheaper.
2. Devaluation of the pound. This makes exports cheaper while making foreign cars more expensive to the UK consumer.
3. Import tariffs and quotas. This will reduce the number of imported cars that can be sold in the UK. If you read the following article you will realise this is true to life:

Car unions unite to fight for import controls

Trade unions throughout Britain's vehicle and car components plants are to unite to campaign for selective import controls. . . . At a meeting in Coventry yesterday more than 100 senior shop stewards set up a committee to co-ordinate the fight against foreign imports, which they say are slowly strangling the home car trade.

The campaign involving unions at BL, Ford, Vauxhall, Lucas and other companies, will seek protective legislation from Parliament. There will also be more immediate direct action, possibly with picketing at docks.

Mr. Bernie Passingham, a senior shop steward at Ford, who chaired the meeting, said yesterday that the time for "pussyfooting around" had gone. If jobs were going to be saved, only strong and unified action could do it.

The pressure group, called Campaign for Import Controls Committee, will be based in the Midlands. It also plans talks with unions in the steel and textile industries, which could affiliate to the campaign.

While negotiations with the government are continuing there are strikes at the two factories because the management have refused to give an undertaking that there will be no redundancies. To help resolve the dispute the parties utilise the services of the Advisory Conciliation and Arbitration Service (ACAS). This body cannot recommend a solution, although it can arrange arbitration and its function is to act as conciliators, persuading the parties to consider every particular solution. Following ACAS's intervention the strike is called off when the management promise there will be no compulsory redundancies and the Unions agree to negotiate with the management about voluntary redundancies among the work-force.

As a result of the production lost because of the strike, the firm shows a substantial loss in its UK car plants and as a result no dividend is issued to shareholders. Some of the large investors are extremely unhappy about this and therefore, at the next Annual General Meeting, they intend to use their powers to seek the removal of some of the Board of Directors.

 Section C

 **Model answers**

Chapter 15

Careful consideration needs to be given to answers for 'short-answer' questions and 'long answer' questions in examination papers of the Background to Business paper of the Secretarial Studies Certificate.

Students frequently spend too long on the short answers. The model answers given in the first section below show you how much (or how little) needs to be written.

The second section covers 'long-answer' questions. In it there are a number of essay-type answers to the questions. The answers are not 'models' and are given merely to show what would be sufficient for a good 'Pass' in the examination.

1. Short answers
Students are required to answer five of the twelve questions.

(a) What is the difference between a sleeping and an active partner?

An active partner is involved in the running of the business, shares in its profits and losses and possesses unlimited liability. A sleeping partner also possesses unlimited liability, shares in the profits and losses but plays no part in the running of the business.

(b) How would a devaluation affect the Balance of Trade?

The balance of trade is the difference between visible imports and exports. A devaluation would improve it because it would make imports more expensive while making our goods cheaper to foreigners.

(c) The French franc is about to be devalued. What effects will this have on a UK holidaymaker?

If the franc is devalued UK holidaymakers will get more francs for their pounds. It will make their holidays in France cheaper.

(d) State 3 reasons for a rise in British Leyland shares.

Any factor which would improve the profitability of British Leyland would cause its shares to rise, e.g.
Successful launch of new car
Devaluation of sterling (it would make exporting easier)
Import tariffs on foreign cars.

(e) Give an example of a 'communication' you would not use a notice board for. Explain why.

I would not use a notice board to discipline an employee because it would be seen by the rest of the staff. This would upset the employee.

(f) A newspaper article commented that 'White-collar workers will exercise greater economic strength in the future'. Who are white-collar workers?

White-collar workers are employees who perform clerical and professional tasks. They are called white-collar because they wear suits rather than industrial overalls. Their unions include APEX and ASTMS.

(g) What is meant by arbitration?

Arbitration is used when the parties cannot solve a dispute and call in a third party. He is the arbitrator and he will recommend a solution which both sides will accept.

(h) In communications what is meant by the grapevine?

The grapevine is an informal method of communication and consists of gossip and rumour.

(i) In terms of ownership to whom are the directors of a joint-stock company responsible?

The directors are answerable to the shareholders at the Annual General Meeting (AGM).

(j) State the main difference between a commercial and a merchant bank.

The former deals with the general public whereas the latter offers services to businesses.

(k) Explain simply what the term collateral means in banking.

Collateral is security for the loan. If the borrower defaults it can be sold.

(l) Is a rise in the Financial Times Index favourable to the investor?

The index reflects all share prices so a rise is generally favourable although your shares could fall in price while all other shares were rising.

(m) What is a premium?

A premium is the payment the insured makes for his insurance policy.

(n) What is the difference between a quota and a tariff?

A quota is a limit on the number of goods that can be imported and a tariff is a tax.

(o) Give (i) one example of a direct tax
(ii) one example of an indirect tax.

Income tax is a direct tax and VAT an indirect tax.

2. **Long answers**
Requiring traditional essay-type answers.

1. Describe some of the problems a sole trader might face in setting up in business.

The first problem for the person starting in business is to raise sufficient capital. She will need this to set up the business; she will need to buy or rent premises, purchase equipment and perhaps engage specialist staff. She may borrow from friends or relatives or perhaps the bank.

Although she can raise sufficient funds to start the business her financial problems are not over. A new business is unlikely to make much profit in the first year. Even if there is a market it will take time to find customers and during this period bills must be paid. Unless sufficient profit is made to cover these (or her initial start-up capital was large enough) she will go bankrupt.

Having survived the financial hurdles the sole trader cannot relax. She may employ staff (being a sole trader simply means owning the business) but she is responsible for decision-making. She is the management. This will involve working long hours and she will find it difficult to take holidays. She may also be forced to work when feeling ill.

Underlying all these problems is the problem of liability. The sole trader has unlimited liability. This means that if her business debts exceed her business assets her creditors can take all her personal assets (her house and car.) The price of failure is very high.

2. Give examples of the types of training provision which might be provided by:
(1) Employee's own company
(2) College of further education.

The most common training provided by the firm is induction training. This is given to all new employees and consists of telling them about the company and its products, company facilities and rules, the nature of the job and finally giving them a tour of the firm. Once the employee has been 'inducted' she may be given on-the-job training. This might involve learning how to use the various pieces of equipment such as photocopier or switchboard. Once an employee has learnt her job, training does not finish. There might be changes in technology which require her to retrain, e.g. a typist learning how to use a word processor. She might be promoted and this might involve her learning new skills, and all the time the company may be running short courses to improve performance.

The retraining for word processing might be done at the local college but the college is mainly used for other types of off-the-job training. This could be for existing employees in the form of day release (this is common in apprenticeships) or it could be training of individuals so they acquire the necessary skills before they start work. This would be the situation of a secretarial course in a college. Colleges also offer short courses for employees who wish to acquire qualifications to improve their promotion prospects.

3. Describe the advantages and disadvantages of putting money into
(i) Stocks and shares
(ii) Deposit account
(iii) Building society account.

The advantages of stocks and shares are that they can rise in value, perhaps faster than inflation. This means that if you invest £500 it might become worth £1,000. While you own the shares you will receive income in the form of dividends, provided the company is making profits. The big disadvantage is that you can lose all your money. If the company makes a loss you will not receive a dividend and if it goes bankrupt you might lose all your £500.

A deposit account in a bank is secure. If you invest £500 you know you can withdraw £500 at any time. You will be paid interest on your deposit but the disadvantage is that your deposit grows slowly. If inflation is high, although you can withdraw your £500 it may be worth less than when you invested it.

A building society account is just as secure as a deposit account and also pays interest. It may also fail to keep pace with inflation. The advantage of this account is that it gives the saver priority when seeking a mortgage. There are a variety of accounts and you can choose one that suits your method of saving. You can have one that allows instant withdrawal or one that requires you to leave in money for some years. This pays a higher rate of interest.

4. Describe 2 ways in which an adverse Balance of Payments may be corrected.

An adverse Balance could be cured if a country reduced its imports. It could do this by imposing tariffs or quotas. The first is a tax on imports and this causes their price to rise. This, it is hoped, will discourage people from buying them. A quota is a limit on the number of items that can be imported. If the government devalues the pound this will also reduce imports because it makes them more expensive.

A devaluation means foreign citizens can buy more pounds for their currencies and so it makes it cheaper for them to buy UK goods. This should improve our export performance. Exports can also be encouraged by the government granting subsidies to firms or by marketing UK goods through foreign fairs etc. The government can also help exporters by trying to persuade other countries to revalue their currencies (which has the same effect as a devaluation of the £) or to remove trade barriers.

The above answers provide an indication of what will prove acceptable in an examination. Just to show what a student can achieve the following answer was written by an ex-student in a mock examination. It is uncorrected.

Q. A car firm has a poor industrial relations record and senior management believe this is caused by poor communications at factory level. In what ways might the communications be defective?

A. The communications in this car firm could be defective for many reasons. One of the reasons for this might be that the management aren't going through the factory supervisor and therefore the factory supervisor is upset because he wasn't consulted so he makes trouble for the management by stirring up the factory workers and telling them that it is a bad idea etc.

Another reason for bad communications could be that the management put up notices on the notice board telling the workers what they have decided and what they want the workers to do, this creates bad feeling as nobody has been consulted. This type of communication, one-way communication, means that they cannot discuss or compromise and management don't see the reactions and feelings of the employees until it is too late to do anything.

If they did get the workers together it could be that they shouldn't have got them altogether at once as this causes the workers to come together as one to argue their points of view.

It could be that the management don't talk to the workers on their level, or that they give the workers too much information to carry out at once causing friction between the two levels. Bad timing is another, if the workers are given instructions or information at the end of the week.

If the management explained the situation, the problems, ideas, they could discuss it and look at each persons point of view and try to sort it out agreeably or compromise, thus make for much better relations.

An example of bad communications is British Leyland over the cutting out of washing up time.

Section D

The project which accompanies the written examination is important because, if well done, it makes passing the examination easier. Students and lecturers often seek guidance from the LCC as to the standards required for each grade. Model projects are available from the LCC but **two** model projects which have been moderated by the LCC follow. It is hoped these will indicate to students the level they should seek to attain.

Project – grade C

Chapter 16

An investigation into. . .
Esso Research Centre Abingdon

A project report required in the Background to Business Section of the London Chamber of Commerce Secretarial Studies Certificate June 1983.

Contents

Report compiled
by
Examination
Number
Name of College
Date completed

Introduction

I have chosen the Esso Research Centre at Abingdon because I think it plays a large and important part in the lives of so many people in all walks of life, not only for people buying petrol for their cars, but for other uses for domestic, factory and testing purposes.

I was able to gain information from a friend who works at Esso and who lives close by. I also went on two weeks' work experience in the Lubricants Division of the Centre and was able to do some work on my project whilst I was there, being accessible to information in the office in the form of booklets, leaflets and brochures, and asking staff certain questions on particular subjects I was studying.

I was interested to find out the different experiments the Centre carries out, and how they affect people in the community and the country.

The Esso Research Centre at Abingdon makes new additives to serve the petroleum industry. It is not a refinery, an office, or anything else, but purely a research establishment for finding new and improved methods for the petroleum industry, although the Centre does have many administrative offices, and other offices in which the staff and scientists work.

The Esso Research Centre has a great deal of confidential information, and spends very large sums of money in their research programmes. They derive much information and develop new ideas which are of substantial value to Esso. This information would, therefore, be of great value to competitors and potential competitors.

History and development

Esso began in 1888 together with the Anglo-American Oil Company and has been very much a part of social and economical development in Britain. The importance of oil is now so great that no one can live without it.

In 1936, Esso set up its first research establishment in the UK. This was called the Vauxhall Laboratories, located on the riverside at London's Albert Embankment. The laboratories were concerned with product quality control work on behalf of the affiliates of Standard Oil (New Jersey) operating in Europe.

From the beginning, the work of the laboratories was continually expanding and when the Second World War arrived, the company accelerated rather than slowed down.

Because of the dangers of bombing during the war, there was lack of space for expansion at Vauxhall so new equipment was installed at Esso House, Abingdon, on an estate owned by Anglo-American.

When the war had ended, there were more facilities for research at Abingdon than Vauxhall, so it became necessary to move the administrative offices, records, library, etc. to Abingdon.

In 1947, the laboratories were set up separately under the name Esso Development Company Ltd.

In 1956, the name was changed to Esso Research Ltd, and in 1967, it became a department of Esso Petroleum and was renamed the Esso Research Centre, the name it has today.

Esso House was originally called Milton Hill House, and during the war, served as evacuation accommodation for Anglo's head office.

In 1970, the company sold Esso House to W H Smith and Sons, the stationers, who use it for training purposes.

In 1958, an important event took place when Lord Hailsham unveiled a plaque commemorating the opening of Building One, housing the main laboratories.

The new building, which also contained offices and the library, replaced several of the prefabricated buildings which had been used for the previous ten years.

EXXON Corporation

Exxon Research and Engineering Company is the oldest and largest research organisation within Exxon's corporate structure. Its main objectives are research, development and engineering activities.

It was founded in 1919 as a wholly-owned, but separately incorporated subsidiary of Exxon Corporation and is responsible for finding, testing and developing ideas of technology to meet most of Exxon's needs in petroleum, refining, transportation and marketing.

Before the Exxon Research and Engineering Company was formulated, another organisation called the General Development Department was formed at Bayway refinery.

About 2,000 scientists and engineers, and a similar number of support personnel, work under the Exxon Research and Engineering Company's management at facilities at Texas.

Research, development and engineering expenditure by the Exxon Research and Engineering company amounted to more than $5 million in 1982. The main funds came from Exxon Corporation and its affiliates. It was responsible for engineering work on more than 50 major projects. The 12 largest of these involved $11 billion in capital expenditures by Exxon affiliates.

The ESSO Research Centre, Abingdon

(i) The function of the Establishment

The British Research Laboratory of Esso is located in a country position on the edge of the Downs about 12 miles from Oxford. It is the largest research laboratory in Europe and its 250,000 square feet of laboratories etc are spread over a 60 acre rural site. It is estimated that the buildings and equipment are worth £25 million.

Esso Petroleum and Esso Chemicals are two separate companies which deal with different aspects of the oil industry, and within the Centre, there is friendly rivalry between the two groups, but which join together at the top.

The main aspects of the Centre's work is concerned with extensive academic, governmental and industrial research. There are many well-equipped general purpose laboratories together with analytical, engine test and pilot plant laboratories in which research is carried out. Subsequently, tests go on into the factories of customers, into ships, into fleets of cars and trucks so that the new products are fully tried and tested before they are branded and available for customers to purchase.

Here are some examples of items that are tested within the Centre:

Additives are one of the Centre's specialities. Work on enhancing oil products by means of theoretical calculations and practical tests at the laboratory bench and pilot reactors. Experimental investigation into how additives work is followed by extensive testing in bench rigs (apparatus designed to simulate parts of an engine), in test engines and in the field. For example, motor oils contain a dispersant, a detergent, a viscosity modifier, and an anti-oxidant.

1. *Dispersant.* Solid, sooty particles which are produced as a result of combustion remain in suspension in the lubricant rather than being deposited in the oil channels.
2. *Detergent.* Prevents the formation of carbon and varnish-like deposits on the pistons or within the cylinders.
3. *Viscosity modifier.* Ensures that the motor oil remains thick enough to maintain lubricating film between surfaces when hot, but thin enough under cold conditions to minimize drag on engines or by restricting variations in viscosity.
4. *Anti-oxidant.* Helps to prevent the oxidation of hot oil by the oxygen from the atmosphere.

The Centre also has many workshops, garages, a printing plant, a photographic studio, meeting rooms, library, offices and a fully equipped cinema/lecture theatre. For the evaluation of automotive products, there is a high speed test track.

The Research Centre exists to provide technical help for Esso companies and through them for their customers. The staff work very closely with the staff of other Esso laboratories, particularly with those in Europe, and with the refineries, marketers and through them with their customers.

The Centre provides technical assistance for Esso Petroleum Company, Limited and Esso Chemical Limited, and it specialises in many different aspects of petroleum knowledge needed for operations, worldwide, of Esso and Exxon. Exxon Corporation is the parent company of Esso Petroleum Company, Limited which is a wholly-owned subsidiary. This specialises mainly in engine lubricants of all types, in gasoline, distillates, aviation fuels and in gas. There are numerous laboratories that specialise in many other areas of the research.

The Chemicals Research, i.e. the Esso Chemical Research Centre, Abingdon, is mainly aimed at producing new additives for lubricants, and this, which is completely separated from the lubricants research activity, enables the maximum possible use to be made of the many widely used engine tests and analytical facilities of the Centre. It also. includes the Performance Chemicals Group who are involved with the development of chemicals to aid crude oil production.

Over the past five years, £11 million has been invested in the erection of new, modern facilities. The Abingdon laboratories now contain the largest engine test house in the Exxon organisation. In 1981, as part of the investment programme, improvements were made to both the inspection and blending facilities on the site.

Environmental monitoring programmes are a regular feature of the Company activities with technical advice from the Abingdon Research Centre.

North Sea oil

Britain's energy has greatly changed since the discovery of oil and gas beneath the North Sea. The nation's economy has changed and so the balance of payments has risen. The Government has provided the opportunity for further investment of coal, nuclear and other energy sources.

The North Sea is one of the most difficult areas the oil industry has to face – deep water, rough seas and very bad weather. Successful development requires huge sums of money, new technological ideas and excellent management skills. Esso Petroleum has the benefit of being able to draw on the worldwide resources of the Exxon Corporation.

Cost of development
The deepest North Sea projects can cost around £5 million each for each well dug and a drilling ship up to £30 million. Esso has invested £2.1 billion in North Sea development by 1980 and this will rise to nearly £3.5 billion by the mid-1980s.

The oil
North Sea Oil is light and relatively free of sulphur and is of high quality. It is not altogether suitable for the manufacture of heavy fuel, lubricating oil and bitumen, so in order to maintain supplies of these

products, some higher value North Sea Oil is sold abroad and cheaper, heavier crudes are imported.

(ii) Number of staff

Altogether, there are 475 members of the Research Centre staff at Abingdon, most of whom are connected with the Esso Petroleum Company Limited. The members either work on petroleum research and technical service or on general Research Centre services. A smaller number of the staff are employees of Esso Chemical Limited and they are concerned with chemicals, particularly additives. Research and technical services are carried out in this section and Performance Chemicals activities.

Other employees are engaged in the Lubricants Division of Esso Petroleum and also in the Fuels Division. These divisions deal with research into fuels and lubricants and also technical service work. Technical support is provided by the Engineering Division, the Analytical Division, and the Information Division. Administration services for the site as well as Safety and Security for the buildings and equipment and personnel fall within the Analytical and Information Division. A few staff are employed to oversee the Employee Relations and University Liaison activities.

Of the staff, approximately 200 are graduates, mainly in chemistry, chemical engineering and engineering. Many skills are represented in the support staff for these graduates.

Apart from the chemical and engineering technicians working in the 50 laboratories of the centre, there are secretarial, reprographic, electrical, library and many other staff, all essential to the completion of the technical work of the Centre.

The role it plays in the local community

The Esso Research Centre donates useful equipment such as chairs to scouts and any suitable items with which they have finished in the laboratories or any other buildings on site. They may aid local charities, and staff in the Centre are encouraged to do voluntary work.

The Centre provides jobs for the local people, especially in the scientific field. As this area is scientifically nucleated with the Oxford colleges, Harwell, Rutherford, Culham and Jet all being research centres, there are more jobs available in this field. It will also provide work for administrative and secretarial workers but mainly for personnel with a scientific bias.

Other offices around the country will also provide jobs for people to work at the refineries and on the rigs in the North Sea.

The Esso Research Centre at Abingdon provides a Nature Reserve in the grounds of the centre which is managed by the Abingdon Naturalists' Society. One of the aims is to encourage wild life preservation and the Society makes great efforts during winter months to protect the animals.

In June 1972, the Esso Research Centre provided five and a half acres of the Centre's ground to the Abingdon Naturalists' Society for use as a nature reserve and a study centre.

This area used to be part of the Milton House estate. The reserve consists of mainly man-made features such as parkland, an old orchard and a copse. However, there has been a natural invasion of wild animals and plants which has made the reserve an interesting place to study.

A large area has been dug out to form a pond, and over 100 flowering plants have been identified.

Members of the public are welcome to visit the reserve but they are asked not to pick flowers or disturb the wild life.

One of the items donated by the Esso Research Centre is a spectrometer presented to a chemistry department of a University.

An event took place as part of the celebration of two years without a time loss injury at Esso, a safety Poster competition was held for local children. Prize winners received gift vouchers and all entrants were given some form of prize.

The Esso Research Centre also made a series of environmental studies using new equipment in order to test water, and air pollution. This survey work of air and water pollution was directed towards maintaining a better awareness of environmental matters.

The Centre also provides jobs on a temporary basis for school leavers wishing to gain experience or for graduates who are employed at the Centre but at the same time, attend a course at college to learn their skill more thoroughly.

Young people can also join the Centre on a Youth Opportunity Programme for a period of time to gain experience in any of the skills covered by the Centre, such as administrative work, engineering, technical and secretarial. These young people then leave the Centre and usually most find good jobs in the skills they have been *practising* within a very short period of time.

Conclusion

Exxon is a multi-National Organisation which has different incorporated companies all over the world. Esso/Abingdon has connections worldwide although it is a very close-knit community with people working at Esso from Wantage, Didcot, Abingdon and numerous other places, all members contributing to worldwide research.

The advantage of Esso as a large company compared to smaller companies is that it is recognised all over the world. Staff are mostly permanent, e.g. there is not a great deal of staff turnover, so it remains open and does not lose money. If it did start to lose money or support, then assistance would automatically be fed in from the Exxon Corporation in the form of funds, staff or equipment.

On the other hand, small companies are not so easily recognised because of lack of support from parent companies so could easily be closed through lack of funds etc.

Project – grade E
Chapter 17

Report on
Laminated Profiles Limited
(as a result of work experience)

Introduction

Laminated profiles is a firm on the Alton Trading Estate. The firm is in
a good position for trading as it is situated near to the by-pass making
the transport of goods by road easier and much quicker. The goods are
sold all over the country and some go abroad.

Structure of the firm

The firm has a working Board of Directors who each have an office in
Factory One. The directors are responsible for all the final decisions
which are made within the firm. They also draw up all the plans for the
firm in the future such as exploring new markets abroad.

The Accounts Department are responsible for recording all financial
transactions of the firm such as purchase of materials for the
production and the sale of the finished products. There are two reasons
for keeping records of this description within a firm. Firstly the
directors wish to know if the firm is making a reasonable profit or
making a considerable loss. They wish to know exactly where money is
being made and where it is being lost. Using this information the firm
can change methods of production to suit the needs of the market.
Secondly the firm is legally obliged to keep records of its finances.
Every year an auditor visits the firm and checks all its financial records
to see if they are correct and complete.

The Sales Department are responsible for marketing the products of
the firm. It is their job to get new customers who will regularly make
large orders. The firm has names and addresses of all their customers.
Every so often to push up sales circulars are sent out to them
advertising big discounts for a limited period. This usually encourages
bulk buying by the customers.

The Drawing and Design Department are responsible for the
drawings required on the factory floor and in the directors' offices. The
drawings are very detailed and show all the various measurements of
the products. They have to be very accurate because if they are wrong
in any way the result is a completely different product is produced to
what is required by a customer. This results in unnecessary waste of
materials, time and perhaps most importantly money.

Factory One

Factory One manufactures Cascalite Translucent sheets on an
automatic production line which requires only a small group of
workers. A worker to clean the wooden moulds after use which is quite
a messy job. A worker to monitor the mixing of the polyester resin
which is sieved to remove any lumps to prevent spoiling the finished

spoiling the finished product. The resin is reinforced with glass fibres. The sheeting is then moulded into the required profile by drawing it through the wooden dies, within a heated oven. The sheeting is then cooled down with water which is sprayed onto it. Finally the sheeting is cut into the appropriate lengths to suit the roofing requirements of the customers. Two or three workers monitor this final process of cutting and stacking up the sheets ready for transporting. The construction of Cascalite provides considerable strength which enables the sheeting to be fixed and handled without the fear of it shattering.

Cascalite is produced in a natural translucent finish which provides natural light for factories, warehouses, agricultural buildings, canopies, car ports, swimming pool covers, vertical glazing, suspended ceilings and partitioning Cascalite is also produced in a colour-tinted finish. Green or blue tinted sheeting is particularly suitable for use overseas in reducing glare in countries subject to bright sunlight.

Cascalite is available flat and can be corrugated in a large range of profiles. Each of these profiles are designed to match in with most types of asbestos cement, aluminium and steel roofing.

Double Skinned Units provide thermal insulation too. Other types provide water absorption, flexibility and hardness depending on the needs of the customer.

Below are some examples of Cascalite Translucent Sheeting

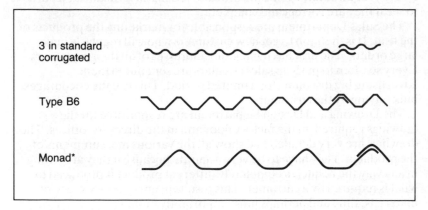

3 in standard corrugated

Type B6

Monad*

Factory Two

Factory two manufactures Reinforced Plastic Poles e.g. telegraph poles. These Lampro poles offer various advantages over the conventional wooden or steel ones. They have a neat appearance and smooth exterior which cannot be attacked by insects or fungi. Indeed they are highly resistant to marine tropical and industrial environments with chemicals in the ground such as sulphates which can rapidly affect steel and concrete. Also when a vehicle crashes into one of these poles the occupants are less likely to be injured or killed and the vehicle is less likely to be damaged. These poles are produced on an automatic spinning machine.

Reception

The reception area was very pleasant with comfortable chairs and fresh green foliage. The staff from the general office dealt with the reception area clients visiting the firm could be helped quickly without leaving the office by sliding back a glass partition. The glass partition was very useful because it enabled the switchboard operator positioned next to it in the general office to deal with clients the other side of it and on the telephone simultaneously.

The general office

The general office was situated next to the reception. The office was quite small but very well organised. Every available space was used to its best advantage.

There were four large desks. One for each of the two secretaries and one for the Sales Assistant. Each desk was situated in a light, airy position next to a window. Strong sunlight could be blocked out by blinds.

There were filing cabinets and a large three-tier rotary file where information and past invoices which are kept on their customers. There was also a card index containing the names and addresses of their customers and a card index containing the names and addresses of their suppliers. These were kept handy for typing invoices and circulars.

Typewriters

There were two electric typewriters in the general office. The typewriters were in constant use. Most of the time they were used to type order sets.

Orders were usually phoned through by the customers and written down on special printed order forms. The printed forms had to be typed up correctly on special order sets as quickly as possible so the factory could start production. The order sets consisted of four coloured sheets, white, pink, blue and green with carbon sheets between them.

The two secretaries would type up the order sets which were then placed to one side ready for checking by the Sales Assistant or the Sales Manager. This is to ensure the production team produce the correct size and type of sheeting which the customers have ordered. Errors cost money and private firms cannot afford unnecessary waste of labour, time or materials.

The secretaries in the general office were also responsible for typing the circulars sent out to their customers.

The switchboard

The switchboard was situated next to the glass partition for reception. It was quite large and modern with four lines available for use at any one time. It had sixteen extensions and all of these were in use. The bottom line of switches seemed to be generally used for ringing up the extensions. Calls were generally switched through on the three top lines to avoid cutting in or cutting off any conversations which were taking place. To help in the selection of vacant switches were red lights which glowed opposite them.

A lot of the firm's business was done by the telephone. Clients would phone through orders easily and quickly. The operator had a very important position because she would be the first person. Clients telephoning would be in contact within the firm. So she needed to make a good first impression by being polite and helpful and speaking in clear, well-spoken voice. Her main aim is to put calls through whether they are incoming or outgoing as quickly as possible because people left hanging on telephones tend to get very annoyed.

The operator had to have a wide knowledge of the firm's products and clients because on rare occasions she had to give information to clients, usually when the Sales Assistant or Sales Manager could not be contacted within the firm for some reason.

The outgoing mail

All outgoing mail was checked in the general office before posting. Unsealed letters were sealed with a clamp sponge. The letters were sorted into two sorting trays. One tray was for mail going to another part of Great Britain and the other tray for mail going overseas. The overseas mail could then be sorted into mail which was going to the same country.

The incoming mail

All incoming mail had to be sorted to see if there was a number of letters going to the same person or department. Then it was promptly delivered by one of the secretaries to the right addressees. Quick delivery of the mail was important because the information in it might be urgent and need the quick attention of the receiver.

The franking machine

All outgoing mail had to be franked using a franking machine. The
letters were pulled through automatically. The stamp or stamps were
printed on the envelopes. When inserting the letters you had to check
they were up the right way and the correct way round for franking.
Thick or large envelopes could not be passed through the machine.
Sticky labels were passed through the machine and then fixed to the
envelopes in the correct position. Mail was franked according to where
it was to be posted. The appropriate cost could be looked up on a
special wall chart. The chart showed costs of sending mail to every
country in the world.

The weighing machine

The weighing machine was used to weigh thick or large envelopes and
all parcels in the outgoing mail. This is because items such as these cost
more to send depending on their weight and size. The electric weighing
machine calculated the cost when the item was placed on its scales.

The supply room

The supply room was situated next to the reception area. It housed the
telex machine and the photocopier because of the lack of space for
office equipment in the general office. There were two large floor to
ceiling cupboards which held various bits of office equipment such as
duplicating paper for the photocopier in various sizes and also much
smaller items such as pens, pencils, rubbers, rulers, elastic bands,
paper clips, staples, liquid paper.

The telex machine

The telex machine was quite an old and noisy model which was due to
be replaced by a modern and much smaller model which could be kept
in the general office. The new model would also be much quieter so it
would not disturb the staff working in the office.
   The machine was in use quite frequently during an average working
day. Messages were sent to the clients and suppliers in Great Britain
and those overseas. Sending telex messages is very expensive so the
messages have to be as short and accurate as the operator can make
them. The messages were recorded on perforated tapes and then sent
out. This was to prevent any mistakes being made in its transmission
such as wrong prices for goods. The operator using this method can
check his/her work thoroughly before it is sent out to the receiver.

Messages can also be received on the machine without the operator being present. An incoming message was indicated by a loud buzzing.

The photocopier

The photocopier was very modern and had various controls to use in the operation of it. The copies could be made light, medium or dark according to which you required. The machine could produce up to ninety-nine copies at one time.

The factory workers often used the photocopier to produce copies of drawings for use on the factory floor. For these drawings A3 duplicating paper was used. The office staff used the photocopier for duplicating letters and plans. Also used for producing circulars to be sent to clients.

Microfilming

All the microfilming was done in the Accounts Department. All the company accounts except very recent ones were on film to save valuable office space. When a past account needs to be consulted for some reason it is far easier and much quicker to find it on film than in a large filing cabinet of paper documents. The accounts were all on film in date order.

The computers

There was a main computer room near the general office. Here a new computer was soon to be installed to control the other computers within the firm. The firm already had several Apple computers. One of these computers was in the Accounts Department and stored on floppy discs such information as the rate of pay of every person working within the firm. Such information had a secret code which had to be typed into the computer before it appeared on the VDU. This was to prevent unauthorised persons looking up confidential information on the computers.

Section E

Press cuttings
Chapter 18

The syllabus specifically states 'Candidates as well as demonstrating knowledge and understanding (of the syllabus), will be expected to be aware, through newspapers etc, of current events affecting the business world. Questions on this background reading can be expected.'

It follows you should read newspapers. Students often fail to do this. You should read a quality newspaper once a week, cutting out articles that are relevant. You will soon get into a routine and acquire an improved knowledge of current business events. The following are articles taken from newspapers. Each is followed, where necessary, by explanatory notes.

You should adopt the same practice because by referring to the main text to make the notes, you are 'revising' throughout the year. By reading the articles you are, of course, revising!

Bank base rate cut

Bank base lending rates are expected to come down by ½ per cent to 9½ per cent today or tomorrow after a clear signal from the Bank of England yesterday.

The prospect of lower interest rates boosted shares and the Financial Times index closed at an all-time high, up 4.2 at 721.3. But the pound fell back, because lower interest rates will make it less attractive for investors to hold.

The immediate reason for the fall in interest rates is the recent strength of the pound. There is a suspicion that the Government's motive is to get sterling down to a level more acceptable to exporters.

Notes:

1. Interest rates are determined by the Bank of England which acts for the government.

2. The Financial Times index is a general indication of movements in shares prices. If it rises and you hold shares this means your investment is probably worth more.
3. If the pound is weaker it makes our goods cheaper to foreigners and therefore makes exporting easier.

A nasty little nudge to expectations

The rise in retail inflation to 4.6 per cent was hardly unexpected, but it does not come at the best time for the Government. This is exactly the point in the year when many unions are first turning their attention to pay claims, and the cost of living is bound to be a factor. Nevertheless, the rise in inflation from its summer low does look, in the short term at least, as if it will be modest. The chances are that the year-on-year rise by Christmas will fall slightly within the Government's budget forecast of 6 per cent. What happens thereafter will itself depend crucially on the wage round, since wages and salaries still account for some 70 per cent of business costs. The depressed state of demand and output suggest that there is likely to be a small further fall in wage increases compared with last year.

Notes:

1. Wage claims are related to inflation.
2. Prices manufacturers charge are related to their costs of which wages are the most important.
3. Because demand for products is low manufacturers do not require labour. Union's negotiating strength is therefore reduced which is why wage increases might be low.

Saudi foreign trade plunges into the red as oil sales fall

Saudi Arabia's foreign trade plunged into the red for the first time in more than a decade during the first quarter of the year as a direct result of the slump in the kingdom's oil exports.

Figures released yesterday by the Saudi Ministry of Finance and National Economy show that visible trade was $290 million in deficit in the first quarter, compared with a $14.6 billion surplus in the corresponding period last year. Exports, which are almost 90 per cent reliant on oil, dropped by over 40 per cent between the last quarter of 1982 and the first quarter.

The Saudis have seen their oil production plummet from a zenith of more than 10 million barrels a day to about 4 mbd currently, while imports have been growing to fuel successive development programmes. A number of leading industrialised countries – including Britain – now have considerable trade surpluses with the kingdom.

Note:

1. Visible trade consists of items you can see (e.g. oil) and the fall in oil exports has resulted in a deficit on the balance of trade (i.e. visibles).

UK travel account back in the red

Britain's travel account was still in deficit in March – but the number of European tourists rose considerably and the account was back in the black for the first quarter of the year.

Latest official figures show that 750,000 visitors came to Britain in March, 16 per cent more than in the corresponding month last year. But some 1,140,000 British travellers went abroad, 3 per cent up on the level for March 1982, and spent £210 million compared with the £200 million spent in the UK by overseas visitors.

British tourist authorities are now anticipating an increase in the number of American tourists – which is likely to be fuelled by the advent of the new People Express cut price transatlantic flights. However, this could be counter-balanced by a drop in French visitors because of the new currency restrictions.

Notes:

1. Tourism is an invisible export when foreign tourists visit the UK. Money flows into the UK.
2. France has made it more difficult for its citizens to travel abroad in an attempt to improve its Balance of Payments.

Respite for textile industry

Negotiations to secure a cut-back in textile imports into the EEC got under way in Brussels yesterday amidst Third World charges that the Common Market was adopting an increasingly protectionist trade stance. But despite these protests it seems that enough Asian and Latin American textile producers are willing to come to terms with the EEC to ensure that the Common Market will get its way.

Note:

1. The EEC is imposing a quota (limit) on the amount that can be imported.

Brazil seeks new loan

Urgent negotiations took place in Washington yesterday to try to raise an additional $2.5 billion in western government loans to save

Brazil from bankruptcy. This would be in addition to the $4.5 billion loan agreed with the International Monetary Fund over a three year period and a further $4.5 billion in new money from commercial banks in this year alone.

Notes:

1. Brazil has a massive Balance of Payments deficit which it has to finance by borrowing.
2. The IMF has already lent money to Brazil.

Banks in accord on shopping terminals

Deep disagreements between clearing banks over the way to bring in electronic shopping have been resolved and the top executives of a dozen banks have agreed to go ahead with point of sales terminals in shops by 1986.

This follows a long debate among the banks about how to bring in electronic funds transfer in shops. It will allow customers to use plastic cards which instantly debit their bank accounts and transfer the money to shop's account using computerised tills.

The banks said yesterday that trials of the new system could start in 1986 and there could be live tests by the end of 1985.

Note:

1. This change in technology could result in banks requiring fewer employees.

Factory without people opens

Britain's first unmanned factory was opened yesterday by the Industry Secretary, Mr. Patrick Jenkin.

It is a £3 million small batch production line at Colchester producing a variety of shafts, gears, and discs in steel, cast-iron and aluminium. The products made by the robots and the computer-run machine tools are genuine, but the factory is initially operating only as a government sponsored show piece.

Pilot projects in peopleless factories were begun nearly a decade ago in countries ranging from Japan to Bulgaria. The British version has taken five years to emerge.

Sir Jack Williams said yesterday, that the factory produced finished components – untouched by hand – over a three day cycle. The old manpower heavy methods involved 10 to 12 weeks of work and about 50 separate handlings of the different small batches of orders.

Future of London as port in balance

The future of the Port of London now rests on the ability of an independent inquiry, meeting tomorrow to find a solution to a seven-week-old pay dispute involving 2,000 Tilbury dockers.

The independent inquiry, under the auspices of the conciliation service, ACAS, and chaired by Professor Sir John Wood, has to find a way of resolving the dockers' claim for parity with white-collar workers.

The PLA chief executive Mr. John Black, has claimed that the strike has cost the port £5 million and that the London docks will never fully recover from the effect. The Transport and General Workers' Union is officially backing the strike and the strikers are not due to meet again until Thursday.

Notes:

1. ACAS is appointing the arbitrator in the dispute.
2. The Union are using the strike as their form of industrial action.
3. The Union involved is a general union.

Metal Box to shed 470 jobs

Metal Box revealed the loss of another 470 jobs yesterday with the closure of its loss making plastic container factory at Bromborough, Merseyside.

The Wirral factory, which makes thermo-formed plastic containers for the dairy and margarine industries is to shut early next January. Metal Box, still Europe's largest packaging group, blamed the losses on the highly competitive UK thermo-forming market burdened with excess capacity. A spokesman said considerable efforts had been made to improve productivity but forecasts for future trading were that losses would grow.

Talks are being held with the four unions involved – USDAW, the shop workers union, ASTMS, the AUEW and EEPTU and in line with group policy all redundancy payments will be more than government requirements. Rowntree Mackintosh, the sweet makers, also announced redundancy plans yesterday, with the loss of 200 jobs out of the 850 maintenance workers at its York factory. Further proposals are under way among 5,000 production workers and 800 office workers which will be announced shortly.

Notes:

1. Job losses involve both industrial and white collar staff.
2. The unions include industrial (USDAW), craft (AUEW), and white collar (ASTMS).

Post Office Engineers widen action against sell-off

The Post Office Engineering Union spread its industrial action against privatisation outside London for the first time yesterday.

The Union also said that its work-to-rule, begun on Monday, by more than 1,000 engineers maintaining international telephone services, was already having an impact. The work-to-rule is affecting three exchanges at Mondale House Upper Thames Street, Stag Lane in Burnt Oak, and Wood Street near Tower Bridge.

After one day of action the union reported 900 faults at Mondale House – 6 per cent of total circuits. Stag Lane and Wood Street are said to have faults on 5 per cent of circuits.

Mr. Keith Simmons, organiser of the union's international servicers branch, said: "We have 100 per cent support within the branch and increasing signs of congestion in international traffic circuits." Management has not taken any action against those working to rule, but it is widely thought disciplinary action will begin soon.

The union has committed itself to a campaign of industrial action against government and big business telecommunications in an attempt to prevent the sale of BT.

Notes:

1. The industrial action being used is a work-to-rule.
2. The government is attempting to 'denationalise' British Telecom by selling shares to the public. This is the reason for the dispute with the union.

Spectacular rise

Mr. Rodney Bickerstaffe, the 38 year-old general secretary of the National Union of Public Employees, has been elected by the TUC as one of its six representatives on the National Economic Development Council, the body which brings together Government ministers and the two sides of industry.

His elevation yesterday to the "Neddy Six" completes a remarkably rapid rise through the TUC hierarchy since he became NUPE general secretary last summer and a member of the TUC general council last September.

Notes:

1. NUPE is a type of industrial union, everyone in the public sector can belong.
2. The TUC is the body representing all unions.

3. The general secretary is the 'head' of the union.

Abbey National breaks home loan cartel

The building societies' long established system of a single mortgage rate for all home owners has been shattered by a decision by the country's second largest society, the Abbey National, to withdraw from the scheme.

The building societies' joint agreements on mortgage and savings rates have been under threat for the past few years, since the incursion of the High Street banks into the home loans market and increased competition for personal savings have breached the near monopoly position the societies previously enjoyed.

Notes:

1. The competition from the banks has resulted in the Abbey National leaving the building societies 'association' so that it can be more competitive.
2. Interest rates offered by building societies to investors and borrowers will now vary between societies.

Rights issue raises £48 m

The rapidly growing financial group Exco International is raising £48 million through a rights issue and using £17 million of it to gain overall control of Telerate, the booming New York firm which supplies computerised data to dealing rooms around the world. Telerate is a rival to Reuter's Monitor service.

Of the rest of the two shares for nine rights issue proceeds, £17 million will be used to wipe $25 million off Exco's US debts and the remaining £14 million will be to broaden the group's capital base to take account of a larger business and further expansion.

Note:

1. One method a public company can use to raise finance is by selling new shares to its existing shareholders (this is called a 'rights issue'). In the above, existing shareholders can purchase two new shares for every nine they already hold.

Index